# USA 2025
## How Republicans Could Take Over and Transform America

Geoff Locander

USA 2025
HOW REPUBLICANS COULD TAKE
OVER AND TRANSFORM AMERICA

Copyright 2023 by Geoff Locander

No part of this publication can be reproduced or transmitted in any form without the permission in writing by Geoff Locander

ISBN 979-8-98747-160-9
eBook ISBN 979-8-98747-161-6

# TABLE OF CONTENTS

Introduction ............................................................................... 1

The Beginning: 2015-16 ............................................................ 3

President Trump 1.0 ................................................................ 14

Trump is Checked .................................................................... 22

President Biden 1.0 .................................................................. 34

2022 Midterm Elections .......................................................... 38

2024 GOP Nominee ................................................................ 46

2024 Democratic Nominee ..................................................... 49

2024 Third Parties ................................................................... 52

Trump 2.0? ............................................................................... 54

Reversing the 20th and 21st Centuries ................................... 57

Senate Filibuster is Busted ....................................................... 58

New House Rules ..................................................................... 60

First Amendment and Free Speech ......................................... 63

Second Amendment and Gun Rights ..................................... 66

United States of Fifty-Four States? .......................................... 68

GOP's Unfinished Business ..................................................... 71

LGBTQ Rights or No Rights? ................................................. 81

Immigration and Citizenship .................................................. 83

Labor Unions ........................................................................... 87

National Election Law? ........................................................... 91

US Domestic Economy ........................................................... 94

| | |
|---|---|
| USA and the World | 97 |
| Federal Patronage Army | 100 |
| Church and State | 102 |
| Who Needs Public Education? | 103 |
| The Strange Death of Democratic America | 105 |
| USA: A Failed Democracy? | 107 |
| Civil War or Succession? | 109 |
| GOP Rule Forever? | 113 |
| Timeline 2023-2027 | 116 |
| US Constitution | 125 |
| Key Supreme Court Decisions | 138 |

# INTRODUCTION

I wrote *USA 2025* to explain what has happened in the United States since the 2016 presidential campaign and what I believe *can happen* in the few next years. The scope of the book's analysis goes back much further, well into the 1980s and even before.

I have no axe to grind. In politics, I'm an Independent, neither a Republican, nor a Democrat.

The thesis of *USA 2025* is that Republicans will regain full power after the 2024 election, winners of the "trifecta": US President, US Senate, and US House. Reinforcing those three victories would be the United Sates Supreme Court, with six GOP appointees and only three Democrats.

By a narrow margin, hurt immensely by the Dobbs abortion decision, the GOP failed to capture the Senate in 2022. The Democrats were lucky in that election, despite high inflation and an unpopular incumbent president, Joe Biden. That good fortune may not hold in 2024.

Donald Trump could be elected president again in 2024, ending his four years in exile. But he may not win the GOP primary. His chances are now less than 40% for renomination. Whether Trump is elected, or another Republican is, I believe that the United States will undergo immense changes in the years thereafter, if under total GOP rule.

Those changes might be as great as America experienced in the Civil War and Reconstruction eras. Both major parties now think that US politics is a zero-sum game. Either you win, or you lose. Neither side believes there are any worthwhile compromises.

## GEOFF LOCANDER

Why should power be divided, forever shifting back and forth? Isn't there a way forward to keep one party, and one way of thinking, always in control? Partisans on both sides want that.

Future projections in *USA 2025* focus on actions which now are constitutional and politically feasible, should the Republicans win it all in 2024.

I have presented, I believe, only well documented facts and logical projections. The book is intended as both history and speculation, a rather unusual combination. As with any author's work, my personal opinions and prejudices may have crept into the writing, but I hope not too much.

Some abbreviations are used which include the names of US states (i.e., AL for Alabama) and a few others. If in doubt, please check on the internet. Readers of this book are likely to be knowledgeable of US political history, so some background facts have been omitted. If not, the book would be excruciatingly long, explaining in depth, American history for the last 150 years or more. *USA 2025* might rival Gibbon's *Decline and Fall of the Roman Empire* or Shirer's *Rise and Fall of the Third Reich* in length, if not in any other way.

My hope is that you will find *USA 2025* readable, engaging and thought provoking. Enjoy!

# THE BEGINNING: 2015-16

Thousands of books or articles have been written about the political career of Donald J. Trump, first as a candidate, then as President and now as an ex-President. In the beginning, most commentors expressed bemusement or bafflement about someone they believed incapable of winning any 2016 Republican primaries, much less gain the nomination. To them it was seemingly a half serious effort, motivated to gain publicity for the Trump brand of hotels, golf courses and products.

Donald Trump toyed briefly with a GOP primary campaign bid in 2011 for the 2012 nomination, but never actually ran. His message focused on then President Barack Obama's alleged non-citizenship. Most voters, beyond the New York City metropolitan area, knew Trump only as the star of a television reality series "The Apprentice." Herman Cain, another rank business outsider, had much greater longevity in the GOP 2012 race. Cain got as far as the GOP primary debates with his catchy "9-9-9" income tax scheme and briefly led in the 2012 nomination polls.

Donald Trump, after announcing his candidacy in 2015, at first seemed more interested in selling "Make America Great Again" (a.k.a. MAGA) merchandise than conducting a real primary campaign. That campaign would require local and state field offices, a professional campaign staff along with massive media spending. Trump would likely have none of them. Certainly, political writers believed, each of those elements were needed to win the nomination.

All the other GOP candidates were, in the eyes of the pundits, infinitely more qualified. Nine were current or former state governors: Jeb Bush, Scott Walker, Chris Christie, John Kasich, Bobby Jindal, Mike Huckabee, Rick Perry, George Pataki, and Jim Gilmore. Four were sitting

US Senators: Ted Cruz, Marco Rubio, Lindsey Graham, and Rand Paul. A firm belief that Hillary Clinton would be the very beatable 2016 Democratic nominee attracted an exceptionally large field of Republican candidates.

Trump in contrast, had never run for, much less won any political office. He had not served in the military and had not been in government. Without that background, no one in the United States had ever been elected president.

The last non-politician to become president was Dwight D. Eisenhower. But General Eisenhower was America's greatest World War II hero, the leader who defeated Nazi Germany. Wasn't Trump's greatest triumph, the joke went, firing Gilbert Gottfried on the "The Apprentice" television show? What else had Trump accomplished, critics said, aside from failing to pay back millions in business loans, stiffing building contractors and sending five of his companies into bankruptcy?

Reasoning went that if Trump stayed in the 2016 GOP primary field, his many flaws would be exposed in the fall 2015 candidate debates. That would be long before the February 2016 Iowa caucus and New Hampshire primary. Wouldn't Trump prove to be an incompetent debater in a high stakes format facing experienced politicians who had honed their skills through many successful campaigns? Wouldn't his suspected lack of knowledge on domestic and foreign policy issues be fully revealed? Wouldn't his brash, some would say ill mannered, verbal style be off-putting to most voters? Was Trump even a Republican? He had contributed money to Democratic candidates and had failed to vote regularly for decades.

But Donald Trump proved the doubters wrong. Trump's in-person performance skills, refined on "The Apprentice", along with his natural charisma (lacking in most other candidates) attracted many supporters. Turning "lemons into lemonade", Trump's corporate bankruptcies were recast as shrewd business moves, which should be envied, not condemned. He said he was worth $10 billion, wasn't that proof enough?

Trump was also helped, as is almost every successful presidential nominee, by good luck. He faced a very large primary field. There were 17 announced candidates. Most of them participated in the 2015 TV debates.

However, roughly half of the candidates were assigned to the "kiddie table" (2nd tier debate group) because each had drawn low poll rankings. Those kiddie debates garnered little TV viewership. All candidates in that sad grouping were to drop out before 2015 ended.

Trump's celebrity status and TV cable channels voracious demand for news content led to a wholly new phenomenon. Hundreds of millions of dollars in free advertising were given to a political candidate's campaign rallies, namely to Trump's. That TV coverage cost the Trump campaign very little, mainly rental fees for rally venues along with air travel. Some of those expenditures were offset by profits on the sale of MAGA merchandise.

To keep campaigning, Trump wouldn't have to raise huge sums of cash from big outside contributors and make himself beholden to them. Instead, Trump raised millions on the internet from small donors excited by his TV rally appearances.

During the 2015 fall candidate debates, few of his GOP opponents focused on him. Trump was at the "adult table" (1st tier debate group) in each and had a prominent place at or near the center. Fame helped Trump enormously, earning him a strong and often leading position in the late 2015 primary polls.

However, the pundits said, the *real* top GOP contenders were Jeb Bush, John Kasich, Ted Cruz, and Marco Rubio. Each one attempted, within the framework of the 2015-16 GOP orthodoxy, to explain why he should be the party's nominee and then would go on to defeat Hillary Clinton in November 2016.

Trump was dismissed as a "carnival barker", a showman without substance. Wouldn't he be just a minor character in the 2016 primary election? Once "Trump Fever" had passed, be forgotten as quickly as Herman Cain was? Yes, both the national media and the GOP establishment agreed.

But Trump differentiated himself in the debates from the 2015-6 GOP orthodoxy, which almost every other candidate embraced.

- No, said Trump, the Iraq War was a major mistake by former President George W. Bush.

- No, said Trump, free trade isn't helping America, but mainly helping China.
- No, said Trump, illegal immigration must be stopped by building a southern border wall, which Mexico would pay for. Obama's "Path to Citizenship" and his "Dreamers" scheme made no sense.
- No, said Trump, NATO isn't working, and Europeans had to pay their fair share for defense and not rely on US tax-payer dollars.
- No, said Trump, the rising costs of Social Security and Medicare aren't real problems. Reducing benefits for retirees or raising the ages of eligibility are bad ideas.

Perhaps most importantly, Trump said the "Washington Swamp" had to be drained. That meant career politicians, which included nearly all his opponents, should not be awarded the Republican nomination.

On February 1, 2016, the delegate selection process began with the Iowa Caucuses. Ted Cruz won the most delegates (eight), but both Trump (seven) and Marco Rubio (seven) finished closely behind. The other candidates won only three delegates.

The first primary was held on February 9 in New Hampshire. All voters could choose either a Republican or a Democratic ballot. In a state won twice by Barack Obama, the GOP primary drew 53% of all voters, despite a spirited Democratic race between Hillary Clinton and Bernie Sanders. Trump won the GOP contest easily, with 35% of the vote. His four major opponents (Cruz, Rubio, Bush, and Kasich) *combined* won barely more votes than Trump.

Later in February, Trump went on to win both South Carolina (primary) and Nevada (caucus). Jeb Bush, often the GOP polling leader in 2014-15, dropped out after the South Carolina primary. On Super Tuesday, Trump was the victor in five of eight primaries, mostly held in Southern states. Cruz led in his home state of Texas and in neighboring Oklahoma. Rubio took only Minnesota. Through the later part of March and April Trump continued to prevail. Marco Rubio suspended his campaign in late April, effectively ending his candidacy. Ted Cruz was seen as the last barrier to Trump's nomination. He drew belated endorsements from many establishment Republicans and their allies, hoping to avoid the inevitable Trump loss on November 8 to Hillary Clinton.

By mid-May the nomination race was over. Both Cruz and Kasich (who won only Ohio, his home state) suspended their campaigns. Not enough donors were willing to spend more money on losing election bids. On July 19 Trump received the votes of nearly 75% of the delegates at the GOP National Convention in Cleveland. He would face the Democratic Party's nominee, former US Senator and former US Secretary of State, Hillary Rodham Clinton.

Hillary Clinton had been the Democrats' presidential heir apparent since 2008, when she unexpectedly lost the nomination, upset by a little-known US Senate colleague, Barack Obama (IL). Obama exploited Clinton's support for George W. Bush's now very unpopular Iraq invasion and occupation. Barack Obama received massive support from Black Democrats, assumed to be a safe Clinton constituency and won the nomination narrowly.

Resigning from her New York Senate seat in early 2009, Clinton became US Secretary of State in the new Obama administration, holding that post until 2013.

When Vice-President Joe Biden decided not to run for the 2016 nomination, Clinton appeared to have little serious opposition in the upcoming primaries. It was widely believed, by pundits at least, that she might win the nomination as easily as Al Gore had in 2000.

But there was a growing under-current in the Democratic electorate, unhappy with the centrist politics of Hillary Clinton and her husband former President Bill Clinton. Labor unions, major Democratic Party supporters, were uneasy when Bill Clinton signed NAFTA (North American Free Trade Agreement) in 1993. Backed by many more Republicans than Democrats, organized labor feared the bill's passage would result in a significant loss of US union jobs to low-wage Mexican workers. Later, that is what happened.

Stung by the 1994 Republican tsunami, which handed the GOP control of both the House and Senate for the first time in 40 years, Bill Clinton moved to the right. The age of big government was over, Clinton declared. "Aid to Families with Dependent Children", a New Deal law was repealed. It was replaced by the more modest and much less expensive "Temporary Assistance for Needy Families Act." No longer, Republicans rejoiced, would "Welfare Queens" drive Cadillacs. Clinton signed the new bill into law, despite the deep reservations of most progressive Democrats.

In 1999 Bill Clinton signed into law another item on the GOP's wish list, the repeal of the 1933 Glass-Steagall Act. The Depression-era law was designed to ensure that banks could never again destabilize the economy by investing in the stock market or in speculative securities. In the aftermath of the ruinous 1929 stock market collapse, thousands of banks failed. Millions of Americans lost every penny in their personal or business accounts.

The "Big Bank" lobby argued that the Glass-Steagall Act was outdated. Wasn't the law over 60 – years old? Hadn't the American economy been radically transformed for the better since then? The lobbyists said the old Act was too restrictive. US banks were unable to compete with foreign banks. Something must be done to correct that.

Big banking played both sides of the political fence. Most Democratic partisans in the financial services industry supported ending Glass-Stegall. Bill Clinton signed the repeal, despite the overwhelming opposition of Congressional Democrats. The 2008 collapse of the US stock market was caused by speculative big bank investments in mortgage-backed securities and by the irresponsible issuance of hundreds of thousands of shaky home loans. The horrific consequences of that repeal plunged the US economy into its worst contraction since the early 1930s.

The 2000 presidential election foreshadowed some of the problems that Hillary Clinton would face in 2008 and again in 2016. A colorless centrist Vice-President Al Gore defeated an equally colorless centrist US Senator Bill Bradley (NJ) and won the Democratic presidential nomination. The 2000 political landscape looked like that of 1988: a healthy economy and a popular outgoing president. George Herbert Walker Bush, Ronald Reagan's Vice-President, leveraged those to win by a convincing a 7.8-point vote margin over Democrat Michael Dukakis (MA).

Gore's 2000 general election opponent was George W. Bush, the sitting and twice elected governor of Texas. George Bush the younger was more charismatic than Al Gore, admittedly a low bar to hurdle. But he lacked foreign policy experience, aside from dealing with neighboring Mexico. Some unkind critics inferred George W. Bush also lacked brainpower. Bush was nominated, they said, because many voters confused him with his father. Big contributions from GOP donors in Texas and other friends of the elder Bush greatly helped "W's" campaign as well.

A wildcard came into the 2000 race, Ralph Nader. Nader was the famous author of "Unsafe at Any Speed" a best seller published in 1965. The book detailed the numerous safety problems of American cars then being manufactured, especially Chevrolet's Corvair models. Nader's book helped to push public demand for a Federal automotive safety law. Standards adopted by Congress in 1966 included mandatory windshield safety glass and seatbelts for all new motor vehicles made in the US.

Nader's attention was now focused on progressive causes. Those included the need for affordable healthcare, free college tuition, a much higher minimum wage, and the reduction of corporate political influence in the US. Those themes were echoed by Senator Bernie Sanders (I-VT) in 2016 and again in 2020.

Campaigning as the Green Party's candidate, Nader said Gore and Bush were nearly interchangeable. It would make no difference to the average American which one was elected. Ralph Nader won almost three million votes and earned a higher percentage of support than any other left-leaning or progressive candidate since 1932. It was generally agreed that had Nader not run, Al Gore would have been elected President.

In the 2016 Democratic primaries Senator Bernie Sanders ran a surprisingly strong race against Hillary Clinton. Sanders won 20 state primaries, or caucuses and took 43% of the popular vote. Most Sanders supporters were admirers of his progressive policies, but many other voters just chose Sanders because of their dislike of the Clintons. Sanders performed well among whites, especially men, in blue collar and rural areas. The Hillary Clinton candidacy was saved by her strength with female and minority Democrats.

In the general election contest, an unusual focus was placed on the supposed personal flaws of both Trump and Clinton. Donald Trump addressed most of his perceived flaws throughout the GOP nominating process. Trump faced a very threatening new revelation on October 8. An "Access Hollywood" television series video was released which recorded him using vulgar language about women's reproductive organs. The tape also suggested that Trump was a sexual predator, perhaps even a rapist. But Trump, seemingly as confident as ever, weathered the storm. It was only harmless "men's locker room talk" he explained at the next presidential debate a few days later. He really didn't mean to offend anyone, certainly not women.

Hillary Clinton had been grilled by a GOP US House panel about her part in the "Benghazi Affair", a terrorist attack on the US diplomatic compound in Libya while she was of Secretary State in 2012. And then there was the matter of Clinton's use of her personal PC server for over one hundred emails sent while she was Secretary of State. These emails contained US government documents including many marked as "Secret" and "Top Secret". Wasn't that illegal? Democrats dismissed these attacks as partisan witch hunting, but they didn't go away. The Sanders primary campaign concentrated on his policy issue differences with Hillary Clinton, and little on the Clintons' political money-making machine.

The Republicans choose not to ignore it. The GOP said the Clintons were political grifters, using office and power to make themselves rich ever since Bill Clinton was elected governor of Arkansas in 1978. Hadn't Bill Clinton made millions of dollars yearly giving paid speeches after he left office in 2001? Wasn't the Clinton Foundation just a scam designed to raise money in exchange for future political favors? When the great day arrived and Hillary Clinton was elected President, wouldn't those chits from donors become fully redeemable?

If Donald Trump had questionable sexual morals, what about Bill Clinton's? Rumors of his extra-marital affairs went back to the 1980s. The Monica Lewinski episode, which helped lead to Bill Clinton's 1998 Congressional impeachment, was simply another example. And, by the way, what self-respecting wife would tolerate years of that kind of behavior from her husband? Perhaps, it was whispered by some Republicans, Hillary Clinton was a lesbian. Just look at those pantsuits!

After the nominating conventions in July, Clinton nearly always led in the general election polls. Her lead fluctuated from tiny to substantial, a high of eight points after the "Access Hollywood" video was released. In the fall-out from the tape, many Republicans, including some 2016 election candidates, tried to distance themselves from Trump and refused to endorse his bid.

But the "Access Hollywood" kerfuffle gradually faded as did Clinton's eight-point poll lead. A new bombshell exploded on October 28. The FBI Director, James Comey, sent a letter to Congress saying that his agency was reviewing more of Hillary Clinton's emails. That revelation further eroded the Democrat's lead in the polls. Just prior to the election on November 8, her margin over Trump was three to four points in the major polls. But maybe that lead might still be shrinking.

Election polling experts generally gave Clinton an 80%-90% chance of becoming America's first female president. After all, with that large a lead in the popular vote, how could she lose? Little heed was paid to statewide polls in Wisconsin, Michigan, and Pennsylvania, where Donald Trump was rapidly gaining ground. It was thought that a Democratic nominee couldn't possibly lose those "Blue Wall" states. None had voted for a Republican presidential candidate since 1988. Even in 2000 and 2004, losing Democratic nominees Al Gore and John Kerry had won all of them.

On November 8, 2016, Donald J. Trump was elected as the 45th President of the United States. It was an upset nearly as shocking as Harry Truman's 1948 comeback victory over Tom Dewey. Clinton won the popular vote, but with a margin far smaller than was expected, just 2.1%.

Many in the now very grumpy mainstream media commentariat complained that the pollsters had missed badly. Their polling methodologies must be wrong. But they weren't. The difference between the final average forecast vs. the actual results (about 1.4%) was well within the pollsters' long-established margin of error. A much greater error would occur in 2020. There will be more discussion of that subject in a later chapter.

A few Democrats called Jill Stein, the Green Party's candidate, a spoiler. Didn't she cost Hillary Clinton the Presidency, they said, just as Ralph Nader had kept Al Gore from winning in 2000? It's true, mathematically, that if every Green Party voter in Wisconsin, Michigan and Pennsylvania had chosen Hillary Clinton and not Jill Stein, Clinton would have won. Of course, that never would have happened.

Overall, in the 2016 presidential election, right-aligned candidates received roughly 50.3% of all ballots cast while left-aligned candidates won 49.7%. Couldn't Donald Trump plausibly claim that the Libertarian nominee Gary Johnson prevented him from defeating Hillary Clinton in the popular vote? Trump did publicly gripe that he really hadn't lost the popular vote. Over three million illegal Democratic ballots had been cast, he said, most of them in California!

The GOP easily retained control of the US House of Representatives, with a net loss of only six seats and pulled in over 51% of the House vote. The US Senate, expected to be retaken by the Democrats, remained in GOP hands. Pre-election underdog Republican US Senators Ron Johnson (WI) and Pat Toomey (PA), were each comfortable winners, substantially exceeding Trump's vote margins in their respective states.

Another GOP incumbent, Kelly Ayotte (NH) wasn't as fortunate. In the wake of the "Access Hollywood" video, Senator Ayotte had withdrawn her endorsement of Trump. In response, Trump angrily suggested that his New Hampshire supporters shouldn't necessarily vote for Ayotte. Some apparently did not. Unlike in almost every other state, GOPer Ayotte did no better than Trump and lost by around 1,000 votes to Democrat Maggie Hassan.

Most important for the future was the shifting political terrain. Obama's 7.8-point victory in 2008, fell back to 3.5 points in 2012. Hillary Clinton's margin was only 2.1 points over Donald Trump. True, the GOP had won the popular vote only once since 1988, but they twice elected presidents (2000 and 2016) with fewer supporters than the Democrats. Al Gore defeated George W. Bush by .7% in 2000. Only 520 more Bush voters in Florida kept Gore out of the White House. Now in 2016, Clinton led Trump by nearly 2.9 million votes and still lost. If that disturbing trend continued, could the Democrats ever again win a close presidential race?

The 2015-16 mini-recession in the manufacturing, agricultural and energy sectors of the economy was a critically important, but a mostly overlooked reason for Trump's victory. Many workers in those sectors lost their jobs and many business owners either closed their doors or fell into debt trying to keep them open. Voting returns in states like Ohio and Iowa reflected that.

Meanwhile, the college-educated (four-year degree holders and up) were moving towards the Democrats. The highly educated had voted Republican seemingly forever. Those voters once were the GOP's bedrock, just as the white working class had been for the Democrats. In 2016 there was a reversal. Aside from race, the most determinative voting predictors now were education and religious affiliation, and not income level. Gender (women more Democratic than men) and marital status (those married of both sexes more likely to be Republicans) were next in importance.

# PRESIDENT TRUMP 1.0

Donald J. Trump appeared to be surprised as anyone by his unexpected victory on November 8, 2016. The GOP won the "trifecta" and in 2017 would control the White House and both branches of Congress. In the House and Senate Republicans were eager to repeal Obamacare, reduce taxes on corporations, as well as on higher income individuals. Federal environmental, health, and safety regulations which they said harmed economic growth, could be ended, or at least curtailed.

Perhaps most importantly, control of the Senate and Presidency meant that Republicans would nominate and confirm conservative Supreme Court justices. The unfilled chair of the late Justice Antonin Scalia would be occupied by a new GOP justice, not a Democrat. Two of the four sitting Democratic appointees (Ruth Bader Ginsburg and Stephen G. Breyer) were over 80 years old. Might one, or both, retire or expire?

Many Republicans who held Trump at arms-length during the campaign now warmly embraced him, seeking cabinet posts or other major appointments. Notably Mitt Romney, the 2012 GOP nominee, interviewed for (although failed to get) the prestigious Secretary of State position.

The transition from the outgoing Obama administration to Trump's new one proved challenging. Little transition planning was done by Trump, or his campaign staff before the election. Meeting with Barack Obama for first time, and in the White House, Donald Trump seemed genuinely awed by the responsibilities he would assume on January 20, 2017.

Trump had another handicap. Unlike his predecessors, Trump had never worked before in government. His knowledge of what a president legally could do, or not do, was limited. Trump had decades of experience running a privately held business (the Trump Organization) with family members and a tight-knit circle of personal loyalists. Becoming the CEO of the USA would be quite different.

Now as President Trump, he would have to contend with the US Constitution's separation of powers. Congressmen and senators are elected by voters in their respective states. He could not compel any to vote one way or another. Supreme Justices are tenured for life and cannot be fired. However, the heads of some federal agencies (FBI Director for example) are appointed and dismissed at will by the president. Other appointees, like the Federal Reserve Board Governors, have fixed terms of office. Most higher-level appointees require the "advice and consent" of the Senate for confirmation.

But a President *does* have considerable independent discretionary powers:

- As the Commander-in-Chief of the Armed Forces, he or she can direct military action, which includes the use of nuclear weapons.
- Make treaties with foreign governments, but subject to Senate approval.
- Issue clemency, whereby someone convicted of a criminal act can be pardoned, or his or her prison sentence commuted.
- Issue "Executive Orders", which had been by every past president in US history save one. The most famous was Abraham Lincoln's 1862 Emancipation Proclamation. But these orders are subject to review both by Congress and the courts. They can be overturned, but seldom are. In January 2022, there was an outlier, when President Joe Biden's COVID-19 vaccine testing mandate for larger companies was vacated.
- Use "Emergency Powers" which are not explicitly granted in the Constitution. This power was first invoked by Lincoln in 1861 to suspend habeas corpus and to arrest prominent pro-Confederates in slave-holding border states under Union control. His action was overturned by Chief Justice Roger Taney, author of the infamous 1857 Dred Scott decision. But the President ignored him,

and the rebel sympathizers stayed in jail. It was said that Taney commanded no troops, while Lincoln did. In 1942 Franklin D. Roosevelt began the internment of over 100,000 people of Japanese descent by using the same powers. His legal right to do so was upheld by the Supreme Court.

Donald Trump often issued executive orders, including ones imposing additional tariffs on the importation of foreign products. Mostly affected were products manufactured in China. Goods from other countries were impacted as well, including some from Europe, Canada, and Mexico. He also issued an executive order, upheld by the Supreme Court, barring travel to the US by citizens of five Muslim countries.

Critics derided Trump's tariffs as a tax on the American consumer. They, not foreigners, would foot the bill when US importers passed along the tariffs by way of price increases. Tariffs, critics maintained, would be of little help in adding new American manufacturing jobs.

The order barring travel from those five Muslim countries was condemned as xenophobic and religiously prejudiced. If travelers from them were a terrorist threat, why wasn't Saudi Arabia on the list? Fifteen of the nineteen of the "9-11" suicide bombers had been Saudi nationals. Over 100,000 Saudi students now studied in American colleges and universities, paid for by Saudi Arabia's absolute monarch, King Salman. And how many of those were fanatical Wahhabis, like the "9-11" terrorists, just waiting for an opportunity to strike again at the great satanic infidel?

Ready or not, Donald J. Trump was inaugurated as America's 45th President on January 20, 2017. His inauguration day speech reiterated most of the 2016 campaign pledges: restoration of US jobs taken by foreign competitors, building back a decayed infrastructure, fighting Muslim terrorism and above all, always putting America first.

The mainstream media hated the speech. Trump's assessment of "American carnage" seemed especially wrong. Wasn't crime in the US going down, not up, as he suggested? Wasn't Trump's vision of the general condition of America far too negative? And what about all those references to God? Wasn't Trump, never a regular church goer, just playing to his Evangelical Protestant voter base and not speaking to all Americans?

Trump claimed that his inauguration attracted the biggest in-person audience ever. Photographs comparing past inaugurations with Trump's indicated this was a far-fetched assertion at best. The comment also launched a four-year long tracking of "lies, exaggerations or misstatements" made by Trump. Those included ones made on Trump's Twitter account, now his favored means of mass communication. Media outlets in the US, Canada and many other countries kept daily lists of the mounting tally. Some said Trump couldn't talk for two or three minutes without telling a lie.

Donald Trump never had a new President's "honeymoon" polling boost. Except briefly around the Inauguration, more Americans disapproved of Trump than approved. After January 2017 his favorability ratings quickly dipped into the low 40s. They remained there, rarely budging, over the next four years.

Popularity might have been more important if the Republican legislative agenda needed the votes of Democrats in the House, or Senate to pass bills. But that seemed not to matter. GOP congressional leaders were principally focused on their version of tax reform called the "Tax Cuts and Job Act." It passed and was signed into law on December 22, 2017. The greatest beneficiaries were large corporations, smaller "pass-through" companies (including those in the real estate and energy sectors), along with high-income taxpayers.

The GOP's next move was the repeal of the 2010 Affordable Health Care Act (a.k.a. Obamacare). In 2009-10 Republicans claimed Obamacare would gravely disrupt the healthcare system. It was a budget buster, they said. Its huge cost might even destroy Medicare. During the 2016 campaign Trump promised, if elected, to enact a new healthcare plan which would replace Obamacare. The new plan would be both cheaper and better than his predecessor's.

A GOP "repeal and replace" healthcare bill was narrowly passed by the House. Opponents argued there was nothing in the replace part that was better than Obamacare. All it would do, they said, was end federally subsidized health coverage for millions of Americans who could otherwise not get affordable insurance.

The Senate vote was on a knife-edge. Two Republican Senators, Susan Collins (ME) and Lisa Murkowski (AK) had joined all Democrats in opposition. John McCain of Arizona, the Republicans' 2008 presidential nominee and a Vietnam-era war hero, would cast the final, deciding vote. Senator McCain, ill with cancer, dramatically appeared at the well of the Senate. He raised an arm and pointed his thumb down. Obamacare was not repealed, at least not for now.

Trump had feuded with McCain for years. Trump suggested that being captured by the enemy, as John McCain had been after his plane was shot down over North Vietnam, shouldn't make anyone special. Being a tortured P.O.W. for five and a half years didn't count for all that much either. To show his disapproval of Trump, McCain did not attend the 2016 GOP convention. John McCain, who voted against Obamacare in 2010, now repaid Donald Trump in full.

In March 2017, FBI Director James Comey unexpectedly reappeared in the national political spotlight. Mr. Comey, it will be recalled, was a key actor at the end of the 2016 campaign. His announcement that the FBI was re-opening the investigation of Hillary Clinton's email server, sparked an immediate dip in her poll numbers.

Many Democrats were bitter, asserting that Comey's actions near the end of the campaign, had caused Clinton's defeat. Most neutral observers felt that Trump had been hurt as badly by the release of the "Access Hollywood" video. Perhaps the FBI's re-opening of the investigation had only evened things out. But might FBI Director Comey, in an act of contrition, try to make amends?

Since mid-2016 the FBI had been looking into possible Russian inference in the current election. Some reports, later known as the "Steele Dossier", suggested that they had and did so to help Trump win. But did the Russians coordinate their efforts with Trump's campaign? Christopher Steele, a retired British intelligence officer, claimed to have proof. It was no secret that the Russian government and President Vladimir Putin detested Hillary Clinton. Under her the US State Department had opposed the 2014 Russian annexation of Crimea and its ambition to do the same in eastern Ukraine.

None of this was yet known to the US public, although the Obama Administration was briefed before the 2016 election. Comey met with Trump in early 2017 and told him of the investigation. On March 20, 2017, Comey testified before the House Intelligence Committee confirming the Russian investigation. During the hearing, Trump tweeted that the FBI told Congress that there was no interference by Russia in the 2016 election. Comey said that wasn't necessarily so. This statement led to his dismissal by Trump later that spring.

Nothing was ever definitely proven to link the Trump campaign to the Russian government. Still, suspicions were aroused. Didn't the Trump Organization have many past and on-going business deals involving Russia, including loans from several unsavory oligarchs? Wasn't there a grandiose new Trump property planned for Moscow which needed Putin's approval?

And what about those rumors concerning the 2013 Miss Universe beauty contest held in Moscow? Donald Trump sponsored and attended the event. Without his wife Melania chaperoning him, Trump was rumored to have engaged in sexual acts with prostitutes supplied by the Russian government. Didn't Putin's spy service (the FSB, successor to the old Soviet KGB) have video-taped evidence? Might Trump be a Russian "asset", who would act (at least in foreign policy matters) at Putin's command?

Trump's problems with investigations hadn't ended. On May 16, 2017, he met with former FBI Director Robert Mueller (2001-13) soon after Comey's firing. Trump believed that Mueller, a conservative Republican, would be a good replacement for Comey. However, there was a statutory term limit for FBI Directors which Mueller had already reached. Mueller did accept an appointment as special counsel. He would oversee the probe of the alleged Russian election interference.

Trump would regret Mueller's appointment. In June 2017 it was reported that Robert Mueller was investigating Trump for possible obstruction of justice in connection with the Russia probe. In October 2017 charges were filed against Paul Manafort and Rick Gates, former chairman and co-chairman respectively of Trump's 2016 campaign.

Michael Flynn, briefly Trump's national security advisor, was also under scrutiny and pleaded guilty in December 2017 to giving false evidence to the FBI. More investigations and inditements followed. Mueller finished his investigations in March 2019. Mueller said in his final report to Attorney General William Barr that while he did not conclude that President Trump committed a crime, he "does not exonerate him" either.

Trump was still determined to prove that he, not Hillary Clinton had won the 2016 popular vote. The "Presidential Advisory Commission on Election Integrity" (a.k.a. Voter Fraud Commission) was created by Executive Order #13799 in May 2017. The commission was chaired by Vice-President Pence, but in fact operated under Vice-Chairman Kris Kobach (Kansas Secretary of State), a rising GOP star.

In Kansas, Kobach tried to demonstrate that voter fraud existed, but had very little success. He did succeed in pushing a Kansas law which disenfranchised tens of thousands of Kansans (most were elderly) who lacked government issued identification. With that to his credit, Kobach's crusade went national. All 50 states, plus the District of Columbia, were asked to turn over their voter databases to the commission. However, only six states complied. The others refused, citing privacy concerns (most databases included Social Security numbers), or were fearful of attempts at voter suppression. In the end, the Commission found no evidence of voter fraud and was disbanded in January 2018. Kobach returned to Kansas, where he would run for governor later in 2018 and lose.

The Democrats now had plenty of ammunition. Didn't Trump's first years in the White House prove him to be a congenital liar and perhaps even a foreign agent as well? And where was the infrastructure bill that he promised and all those good paying factory jobs he'd bring back? How could someone like that be President of the United States? Shouldn't Trump be impeached, convicted, and removed from office? That was the Democrats' brief against Trump.

The mid-term 2018 Congressional elections suggested that the American people might agree. The Democrats had a net gain of 40 US House seats, enjoying their best increase since the 1974 Watergate-era election. Impressively, the House popular vote swung nearly nine points in favor of the Democrats. The GOP did gain Senate seats in North Dakota, Indiana, and Florida. Those first two were Republican states. Democrats only won them in 2012 because the GOP had nominated so-called extremist candidates, who many otherwise Republican voters did not support. However, Florida was different. Long time moderate Democratic Senator Bill Nelson was upset by outgoing GOP governor Rick Scott. If Florida was a swing state, it didn't seem to be swinging quite the way the rest of the country was. Might that be troublesome for the 2020 Democratic presidential nominee?

Republicans could take comfort that they now had 53 seats in the Senate, rather than 51. The increased margin would make it even easier to confirm new Supreme Court justices. But losing control of the House meant that no partisan GOP legislation would be passed by Congress. Democrats would control every committee of the lower chamber. Many of those committees would be eagerly investigating the Trump, his family and business associates.

# TRUMP IS CHECKED

Donald Trump knew he'd be in for a difficult two years with the House now controlled by the opposition. But perhaps he didn't realize how rough they would be. Democrats began issuing subpoenas and launching investigations shortly after the new Congress was sworn in. These focused on three main areas: 1. possible foreign interference in the upcoming 2020 election, 2. possible illegal business dealings by the Trump Organization and 3. Trump's tax returns.

The election interference investigation queried if Trump was soliciting foreigners again to help in his next campaign. A House committee concluded that Trump withheld military aid to Ukraine (a prospective NATO member) to force that country to announce a phony investigation of Joe Biden and his son Hunter.

A generally discredited conspiracy theory claimed that the Ukrainians, not the Russians, were behind any 2016 election interference. Whether true or not, the key was the testimony of US Army Colonel Alexander Vindman. He was a military attaché in Kiev, Ukraine serving with the American diplomatic mission. Vindman was on the so-called smoking gun telephone call with Ukraine President Volodymyr Zelensky and Donald Trump. On that phone call Trump said, according to Vindman, that military aid would not be released until Zelensky announced the Biden investigation. That incident was the basis of Trump's impeachment in December 2019 for Article One "Abuse of Power."

Article Two of the impeachment was for "Obstruction of Congress", related to the Trump Administration's non-cooperation with various House inquiries related to the incident. The House approved both articles, sending them to the Senate for trial in January 2020.

Non-partisan observers wondered why they bothered. There was no chance the Republican controlled Senate would convict Trump on either article. The observers contended this was an exercise as silly as Bill Clinton's impeachment trial in 1998. Not only would Trump escape conviction, but the trial might even win him sympathy. The GOP narrative of Trump's persecution would be believed more than ever.

Donald Trump was acquitted on both articles. Only Mitt Romney, the newly elected Republican Senator from Utah, voted to convict on Article One. No other GOP senator joined him.

Something very sinister would soon dominate American politics and life for the rest of 2020. In late 2019, rumors began surfacing of the emergence of a deadly new flu-like virus in China that later was named COVID-19. The epicenter was said to be in Wuhan, a city in the central part of the country.

The cause, the Chinese government said, was transmission from diseased animals sold in the city's food markets. Some outsiders suggested there might be another explanation. Was it a coincidence that China's principal viral disease laboratory was in Wuhan? Couldn't negligence, on the laboratory's part, have led to this new virus's escape and then the infection of humans? It would never be conclusively determined which theory was correct.

On January 9, 2020, the World Health Organization (WHO), announced the existence of an unknown new virus-related pneumonia in Wuhan, China. The virus appeared to be spreading quickly to other nations. On January 21, the first US COVID-19 case was revealed by the Center for Disease Control (CDC). It had been detected in a person returning from Wuhan.

By February, confirmed COVID-19 cases were rapidly mounting across the US, first on the West Coast and then in large cities in the Northeast and Midwest. In February the US stock markets took notice. Shares plummeted, eventually losing over 30% of their pre-COVID-19 valuations.

In March "lockdown measures" began, as many US cities and states prevented most retail businesses from operating for fear of the virus's spread. Those entities deemed essential, such as banks, grocery stores, gas stations, and a few others were spared and stayed open. Patrons were required to wear medical face masks (then in very short supply) to enter. But most retailers, such as department stores, beauty salons, car dealerships, and restaurants were shuttered and remained so for months.

White collar employees were fortunate, provided they could work remotely from home via the internet. Most could and they kept their jobs. But service workers, many employed in the low-wage restaurant sector, weren't as lucky. Unemployment exploded. Over seven million American jobs were lost in less than two months. It was projected that unemployment might reach or exceed 15%, a level not seen since the Great Depression of the 1930s.

In Congress, an enormous stimulus bill named the "Coronavirus Aid, Relief, and Economic Security Act" (a.k.a. CARES) was passed unanimously on March 27. The bill infused $2.2 trillion into the US economy. It provided at least $1200 in cash to most working or retired adults, $350 billion in forgivable small business loans, and $500 billion in loans for large corporations. Local and state governments would get $340 billion more to keep them afloat as tax revenues were expected to shrivel.

The CARES Act also gave protection to homeowners and renters. They could not be foreclosed on or evicted, so long as the legislation was in force. The most controversial part of the CARES Act turned out to be enhanced jobless benefits.

Those out-of-work would not only receive insurance benefits from their state's funds, but $600 more each week from the federal government. A jobless $250 weekly earner could now almost triple his or her previous wages by staying unemployed. And wouldn't many be living rent free as well? Logically, why would any of them look for a new job, Republicans asked.

By late spring, initial COVID-19 fears were ebbing. The number of deaths and hospitalizations levelled off and finally receded in the late summer. Mortality was concentrated among the elderly, especially the very old. The US had suffered many more deaths, proportionately, in the Spanish Flu epidemic of 1918-19. The new pandemic was not remotely as dangerous as the 14th century Black Plague. In Europe the population had fallen by a third. The apocalypse was not now.

Later in spring more re-openings were allowed, such as for dental offices, barber shops and movie theaters. Closed restaurants again greeted diners, but with many health restrictions. In some states there were never any business closures or "mask-mandates." Life went on as before. That is until COVID-19 spread from large urban areas to everywhere else in the nation. Even then, there was much resistance to any anti-COVID-19 public health measures. It grew ever stronger, despite an upswing in new cases during the fall. The virus had created an ideological divide: elective mask wearers were likely to be Democrats, while mask resisters were likely to be Republicans.

The COVID-19 pandemic erupted near the start of the 2020 election campaign. Donald Trump was assured of the GOP nomination. But who would win the Democratic primary and face-off against him in November? The most prominent early contenders were Senator Bernie Sanders (VT), Joe Biden (DE) formerly Obama's Vice-President, and Senator Elizabeth Warren (MA). Sanders and Warren belonged to the progressive wing of the party. Biden was a centrist establishment Democrat who seemed to offer nothing new, only a familiar name and face.

A 2nd tier of hopefuls included former South Bend (IN) mayor Pete Buttigieg, an openly gay candidate with a husband. He was joined by Senator Amy Klobuchar (MN) and former US Congressman Beto O'Rourke of Texas. Later mega-billionaire Michael Bloomberg, once a New York City mayor, announced his candidacy.

The first two February caucuses (Iowa and Nevada) and the New Hampshire primary suggested that Joe Biden's political career might have reached its expiration date. Biden lost all three, not exceeding 19% support in any state. Sanders won each. Pete Buttigieg surprised most observers by running a close second to Sanders in Iowa and New Hampshire. The biggest loser, aside from Joe Biden, was Elizabeth Warren. The torch of the party's progressive wing was again being carried by Bernie Sanders.

Before the next primary in South Carolina, the race quickly pivoted. US Representative James Clyburn, the House Whip, endorsed and campaigned for Joe Biden. He feared that if Bernie Sanders were the nominee, Donald Trump would be elected again. The long-time congressman remembered the disastrous 1972 nomination of Senator George McGovern (SD) who was convincingly portrayed by President Richard Nixon as a radical. Vilifying Sanders would be even easier. Didn't he say in public that he was a Socialist?

Jim Clyburn was African American, as were most of South Carolina's Democratic primary electorate. His endorsement was effective. What might have been a narrow Biden victory, turned into a nearly 30-point rout over Sanders. On Super Tuesday, just three days after South Carolina, the shift was confirmed. Biden won every Southern state, helped in each one by overwhelming support from Black primary voters. In New England, Sanders even lost Maine and Massachusetts to Biden. Sanders scored victories in only four states: California, Colorado, Utah, and Vermont.

The nomination campaign was nearly over. Biden would go on to win almost every contest after Super Tuesday. Opinion polls conducted of Democrats during the primary season showed that a candidate's perceived electability versus Donald Trump, more so than ideology, was foremost in their minds. That factor would determine which candidate most primary voters would select. Democrats concluded Biden was a much better bet to defeat Trump than Sanders. On April 8 Bernie Sanders dropped out and endorsed Joe Biden.

The 2020 presidential campaign would be the strangest in modern US political history. Fear of COVID-19 cancelled large outdoor rallies, an erstwhile staple. In previous presidential election years, candidates crisscrossed the country, often holding two or three events each day. Those went away in 2020.

COVID-19 created another Republican vs. Democratic divide – how to vote. Slowly but surely, citizens were casting an increasing percentage of ballots before election day. The main motivation in years before had been to avoid a long wait in line to cast a vote on polling day.

Pre-election day voting fell into two broad categories: 1. absentee voting by mail, which most states allowed (although many imposed significant restrictions) and 2. early voting in person at a polling place. This was permitted by many states, but fewer than those with absentee balloting.

Wide-spread absentee voting was new in the US. Much earlier (pre-1990), it was usually restricted to voters who would be out-of-town on election day. The prospective voter had to appear at his or her city or county clerk's office and apply for a ballot. Those ballots were rarely requested. No exceptions were made for voters who because of illness, or disability, were unable to come in person to their local polling places.

The Florida GOP, eager to ensure that the votes of their elderly supporters would be cast, was among the pioneers in the expansion of absentee voting. Many states followed Florida's lead. In some, there were now no restrictions. In those states everyone could cast an absentee ballot. No explanation or excuse was needed. For a few states, including political opposites like Oregon and Utah, there were no election day polling locations. All votes were cast by mail.

Democratic governors, mayors and other officials clamored for the expansion of both absentee and early voting. They explained that in the COVID-19 world of 2020, no voter should have to stand in line and risk infection. This was, as it will be remembered, before any protective vaccines existed.

But Republicans pushed back and asked why. Wasn't absentee voting potentially fraud-ridden? Some Democratic jurisdictions, Republicans said, now were sending unrequested applications for mail-in ballots to every registered voter. There were many where all voters were solicited to vote absentee. Who could say that in Democratic strongholds like Chicago, Los Angeles, or Philadelphia there would be a fair count? Late mail-in votes would even be tallied, in most states, days after the election was over. Old-fashioned ballot-box stuffing might be back, now in 21st century style!

The 2020 presidential election recorded the highest turnout since the late 19th century. That was a time when most women, Blacks and other non-whites couldn't vote. The majority of 2020 Democratic votes were cast absentee, or early. Republicans dominated in-person voting on election day.

The Democratic presidential campaign was conducted by Joe Biden largely from the basement of his home in Wilmington, Delaware, via the internet. He rarely left. Trump was much bolder and scheduled rallies at small airports. At those events he never wore a protective face mask. After the election, many Democrats would complain of Biden's "hunkered down" campaign. That not only hurt in the presidential race but was copied by Democratic candidates throughout the US to the regret of many.

Another element in the election contest was civil unrest in the wake of the death of George Floyd in Minneapolis, Minnesota on May 25, 2020. Floyd, a Black man, died at the hands – or rather the knee – of a white police officer attempting to subdue him. Protests and violence exploded in cities across the country.

Most Americans, of all races, were at first sympathetic to the Black Lives Matter movement (BLM) after Floyd's death. BLM began in 2013 after the acquittal of George Zimmerman who killed a Black teen, Trayvon Martin in Florida. Most 2020 protests were peaceful, but some criminals exploited them, looting stores, and destroying other property.

A new slogan gained currency among progressive Democrats: "Defund the Police". It wasn't entirely clear what that entailed. In practice defunding usually meant fewer police officers would be on the beat and that police departments would receive less money. Missing street cops would be replaced by community "out-reach" workers. They would use intervention and persuasion to prevent violence instead of brute force. Republicans called the idea crazy. They said it would lead to crooks and street gangs running wild.

Donald Trump and Joe Biden met in only two debates. Another was cancelled because Trump had been diagnosed, later hospitalized, with COVID-19. On September 29 a very cranky Donald Trump debated Joe Biden in Cleveland Ohio. Incumbent presidents have always disliked sharing the stage with their opponents and having to answers questions which they didn't care for. George H. W. Bush hadn't in 1992, and neither had Barack Obama in 2012.

During the first debate, Trump repeatedly interrupted Biden as he was answering questions or even responding to Trump. At one point Biden memorably told Trump, "can't you shut up man." Media commentators and the public panned the debate. Many said it was the worst in history. At the last debate on October 22, Donald Trump was much less petulant. The revised technical format of the debate (remotely controlled microphone on-off switches) made interruption of the other candidate almost impossible, leading to more civil exchanges. Observers believed Trump might have won back some of the ground he lost after the first debate.

Biden's polling lead over Trump was much larger, seven to nine points on average, than Hillary Clinton's had been in 2016, generally three to five points. There was much less volatility than in 2016. Biden's numbers rose slightly after the first debate and fell slightly after the last. Pollsters had another advantage versus 2016: most votes would be cast before election day. Voters could now be asked who they *had* voted for, rather than who they *intended* to vote for. Therefore, poll forecasts should be much more accurate. Or would they?

In Congress, Democrats seemed poised for another excellent year. Generic polling for House races gave them roughly the same margin they had over the GOP in 2018, eight points. Retirements of Republican congressmen in swing districts indicated that Democrats might even increase their majority and perhaps add five to ten seats.

The Senate was very likely to return to Democratic control. The party was expected to win at least three new seats, likely gaining those in Arizona, Maine, and North Carolina. The two seats in Georgia (one a special election to fill a two-year vacancy) appeared up for grabs. Only the contest in deep red-state Alabama was likely lost, as a less controversial GOP candidate would be on the ballot (Tommy Tuberville), rather than Judge Roy Moore. With Biden as president, even a modest three seat net gain would give Democrats control of the Senate.

Donald Trump warned again, as he had in 2016, that he might not accept the results if Democratic chicanery denied him victory. He was even more emphatic in 2020, as he echoed the complaints of Republicans across the country concerning potential mail-in vote fraud.

On election night the expected Democratic landslide failed to materialize. The GOP was winning House seats, not losing them. In the end Republicans netted 13 seats, to cut the Democrats' margin of control to nine seats, rather than 35 after the 2018 election.

Senate GOP incumbents won, save for Martha McSally (AZ) appointed to John McCain's seat after his passing. The Democrats still had a flicker of hope to win Senate control. In Georgia, state law requires that a candidate win 50% or more of the vote, not just a plurality, to be elected. If none did, then a run-off election would be held on January 3, 2021, between the top two vote-getters in any race. Both of Georgia's seats, it turned out, would go to a run-off. On November 8 the two Republicans did a bit better than their Democratic opponents, but the margins were slim.

Who won the presidency wasn't clear. Was the 2020 election going to be a repetition of 2000? On election night, as votes were still being tallied, Trump claimed victory. He said no more votes should be counted, at least not in those states where he was now leading. But the vote counting went on.

The White House winner hinged on the very tight returns in Arizona, Georgia, Michigan, Pennsylvania, and Wisconsin. By Thursday November 5, it appeared Biden would win enough electoral votes to replace Trump.

But the GOP said that something strange was happening. Biden's vote margin was growing daily. Mail-in votes, which were still being counted, strongly favored Biden, usually by 70% or more. Might many of those votes be fraudulent?

Joe Biden won the popular vote comfortably, with a final margin of 4.4%. This was an improvement over Hillary Clinton's 2.1% but fell way below expectations. It was said the pollsters had really missed this time, well beyond an acceptable margin of error.

Why? Methodological reasons focused on the difficulty of getting people to answer pollsters, by telephone or via the internet. In 2020, a hundred people might have to be contacted to get one to respond! That could surely make any poll less accurate. Still, in 2018 the polls were spot-on in predicting the final margin of the House vote. What possibly could have changed in two years?

Conservative media outlets (Fox News and others) said many Trump voters were "shy." Somehow fearful of a survey-taker's condemnation, they wouldn't reveal their true preferences. There might be some truth to that. Republicans were generally less likely to answer political poll surveys than white Democrats or Independents. But so too were many minorities, including African Americans and Latinos.

There was a far more plausible explanation: Republicans worked harder and far more effectively than did the Democrats. The GOP registered millions of new voters. They also combed out those already registered but were inactive. Many Trump supporters hadn't participated in the 2016 election. Republicans were to get both groups to the polls in November. Rather than hunkered down at home, relying on absentee ballots like the Democrats, Republicans campaigned on the ground in traditional ways. That nearly won Trump re-election.

But not quite. In every closely contested state the final tally was apparently won by Joe Biden. Just 44,000 more Biden votes separated the contestants from an electoral vote tie, which would have sent the election to the new House of Representatives. Many of these ballots were recorded after November 3. Tens of millions of absentee ballots had been cast. Weren't those voters strongly pro-Biden? How many of them were fake, cast illegally by the Democrats? Trump said he won re-election and would keep on fighting.

The drum beat of voter fraud grew louder as certification dates for states' electors drew nearer. Trump began pressing Republican officials in GOP controlled states where Biden had won. In Georgia, Trump was taped as asking the secretary of state, Brian Kemp, to "find 11,780 more votes" to send Georgia into the Republican column. Manhattanite Trump might have confused Kemp with a 19th century Tammany Hall sachem. In any event, Kemp refused.

The usually routine electoral certification process became partisan. Statewide vote counts in presidential elections had been seldom disputed since Tilden vs. Hayes in 1876. Nixon versus Kennedy in 1960 and Gore versus Bush in 2000 were the two rare exceptions. GOP supporters increasingly agreed with Donald Trump. *The 2020 election had been stolen by the Democrats and Trump really won!*

In late December Trump met at the White House with House "Freedom Caucus" Republicans. How could the new Congress prevent Biden from being certified? The Democratic controlled House would certify Biden. But the Senate would still be held by the Republicans, with Vice-President Mike Pence as the tie-breaking vote, if needed. If that body chose not to certify Biden, might not the Supreme Court choose the winner?

In 2000 the Supreme Court (with five Republican justices and four Democrats) decided in favor of George W. Bush in the disputed Florida vote count. Now there were six Republicans and just three Democrats on the court. The legal questions were somewhat different than those from the 2000 election. Still, a Republican Supreme Court could determine Trump was the winner, not Biden.

Trump encouraged his supporters to mobilize and join him at a rally in Washington, DC on January 6, 2021. The event was scheduled for the morning, just before both bodies of Congress would meet to certify the 2020 results. Speaking at the rally, Trump declared he would be going to Capitol Hill (which he did not do) and asked his raucous audience to join him.

Many rally-goers did. Several thousand protestors stormed the Capitol building, broke in and forced representatives and senators into hiding from the assault. Policemen were attacked and injured. A Confederate flag was paraded inside. What Jefferson Davis never achieved in almost four years was accomplished in only a few hours by a civilian mob.

Most Americans were horrified. The United States was the world's shining light of democracy. How could this happen here? Surely America in 2021 wasn't Europe of the 1930s, or some Third World country. Or maybe it was?

Soon afterwards, the House voted to impeach President Trump for a second time. In January 2021, the impeachment charge was for incitement of insurrection. Trump was to leave office in a week. Biden's election had been certified by both the Senate and the House. But Donald Trump, if convicted by the Senate, could never legally serve again as president. Fifty-seven senators voted for conviction. Just seven Republicans joined all 50 Democrats. It was not enough. Sixty-seven votes were needed. Trump could again be the GOP nominee and reclaim the White House in 2024.

# PRESIDENT BIDEN 1.0

In an unsteady, but hopeful America, Joe Biden took office on January 20, 2021. Unlike any out-going president within memory, Donald Trump did not attend the inauguration. The country seemed relieved that the histrionics of the past four years might be over.

There now were two FDA approved COVID-19 vaccines available. At first it was difficult to schedule the "jab." Even vulnerable senior citizens waited. By late spring most adults could be vaccinated without much delay. Better yet, COVID-19 infections and deaths were declining.

In Congress Democrats went to work, passing yet another COVID-19 relief bill with a $1.9 billion price tag. Its contents were generally like those before, cash to most Americans, extended unemployment benefits ($300 per week), and more money for state and local governments.

Republicans objected. The COVID-19 crisis was over they said. Unemployment was falling and the stock market had fully recovered. Weren't the Democrats fighting last year's war? The bill was far too expensive and peppered with a left-wing wish list. No Republicans in the House or Senate supported the bill.

Joe Biden was modestly popular in his first few months. His approval ratings were over 50%, but not by much. It was hardly the "honeymoon" that most in the past had enjoyed.

The Democrats' ability to pass more partisan legislation was in doubt. House Speaker Nancy Pelosi, a savvy and skilled politico, encountered trouble from the left-wing of her caucus. Their most prominent face was leader of "The Squad", Alexandria Ocasio-Cortez (NY). Progressives said the popular new 2021 Infrastructure Bill, which had been approved by the Senate, wouldn't be passed by the House without their support. Passage had to be tied to other pieces of legislation they wanted. The leftists commanded enough votes, it seemed, to kill the bill.

In the Senate, Democratic Majority Leader Charles Schumer (NY) had no margin of error with 50 Democrats and 50 Republicans in the chamber. Vice-President Harris could break any ties, but Schumer needed every Democratic vote. Two Senators, Kyrsten Sinema (AZ) and Joe Manchin (WV) were moderate Democrats. Both supported the COVID-19 Relief and the Infrastructure bills but had concerns about other legislation on their leadership's agenda.

Meanwhile Republicans in several states, including Georgia and Texas, were revising their election laws. Revisions were needed, the GOP said, to prevent future voting irregularities and fraud. Democrats said the real reason was to suppress the participation of their supporters. In Texas and Georgia those voters were mostly racial minorities, Black and Hispanic.

Incensed, Congressional Democrats demanded legislation to reverse these so-called suppression laws. But the slope was slippery, and the federal government rarely interfered with state election rules. In 1993 Congress passed the "Motor-Voter Act", which allowed anyone getting a driver's licenses to register as a voter. The bill had some GOP support and wasn't filibustered. That was the last time Congress intervened.

In August the House passed, along partisan lines, a bill named after the late civil rights crusader and Congressman John Lewis (GA). The bill would allow the Justice Department again to overturn discriminatory state laws. It would return many Southern states to the federal tether, removed in 2011 by the Supreme Court. The chances of the bill's passing were nearly zero, as both Manchin and Sinema were opposed. If somehow it were passed, the conservative Supreme Court would surely over-rule and invalidate it.

Still, the Democratic leadership pressed on. An allied and equally doomed measure was filibuster reform. That reform would mean that Senate Democrats could pass any bills they chose by a simple majority.

Senators Manchin and Sinema were again opposed, so filibuster reform never happened.

Elsewhere, Biden was withdrawing US troops and dollars from Afghanistan. Most Americans believed America's over 20-year stay in that country had been a blunder. Hundreds of billions of dollars were squandered and thousands of American servicemen and women were killed or wounded.

A corrupt band of Afghani politicians and generals had siphoned off much of the aid. Only US air power and money kept the Kabul government from collapsing. When American help was gone, the regime it supported disappeared as well. In less than three months, the Taliban was amazingly back in power. With scenes recalling the fall of Saigon in April 1975, thousands of Afghanis who had worked for the US military tried to flee. It was a worldwide embarrassment.

The fall of Kabul was soon matched by a fall in Joe Biden's approval ratings. Quickly he went from the lower 50's in polls to the lower 40's. His approval rating was no higher than Trump's had been at the same point in his presidency.

Something else was hurting Biden – inflation – the highest since the early 1980s. Price increases were everywhere, especially for food, fuel, vehicles, and real estate. Liberals contended that inflation would soon go away, it was generated mostly by supply chain issues and pent-up demand from the 2020 lockdowns.

Conservatives said no. America was awash in sea of green – too much money was chasing too few goods and services. The huge COVID-19 stimulus bills dating back to March 2020 were the culprit. Most Americans agreed. For the first time in nearly a decade, pollsters recorded a plurality of voters favoring GOP control of Congress.

Many observers felt that Biden looked in the mirror and thought he saw Franklin D. Roosevelt, or Lyndon B. Johnson. Biden won the Democratic nomination and then the general election by campaigning as a moderate. Yet once in the White House, he operated as if Bernie Sanders or Elizabeth Warren were the victor. Most of the slippage in Biden's approval came from middle-of-the-road Democrats and Independents who had supported him in 2020.

The Democrat's evil lodestar, Donald J. Trump who generated so much passion, had seemed to vanish. Without the bogyman of Trump to frighten their voters, Democratic politicians went into the 2022 mid-term election uncertain and afraid. A few tried to whistle past the graveyard. Most feared the certain beating which seemed to await.

# 2022 MIDTERM ELECTIONS

Storm warning flags were waving briskly against Democrats in late 2021. Virginia, which Biden had won by 11 points in 2020 voted for Republican Glenn Youngkin as its next governor. In New Jersey the incumbent Democrat barely won his re-election bid. That was a state which Biden had carried by nearly 16 points.

Joe Biden's early 2022 approval ratings showed no improvement from late 2021. The arrow continued to point downwards. Republican favored issues of inflation, crime and border security were dominant in the minds of most voters. The stock markets had defied economic gravity since mid-2020 rising to record levels at the end of 2021. Many investors with hefty portfolios had never been richer, at least on paper. But that changed in 2022 and by the end of the year stock indices were markedly depressed.

The prices American consumers paid for products or services kept increasing. Home values rose at their fastest historical rate as Federal Reserve policy kept borrowing for mortgages at near record lows. Broad spread COVID-19 related remote working did the rest. If people could live in a less expensive, bigger, and nicer property, why not move? Millions of white-collar workers, especially those living in pricey big cities, came to this conclusion. As a result, housing prices soared at incredible rates in smaller metropolitan and rural areas. Bidding wars were common, and many new purchasers paid a premium well above the original list price.

Not everyone was a homeowner or could work remotely. These were largely voters who had strongly favored Biden over Trump in 2020: younger, poorer, and more likely to be persons of color. As housing prices rose, so did those of rental units. There was some lag, as most renters have year-to-year leases. But by mid-2022 renters began feeling sticker shock.

Automotive prices skyrocketed. New cars, mostly because of COVID-19 supply chain disruptions, were very hard to find and often required entering a long waiting list to obtain a vehicle. Big dealerships, which once had hundreds of units on their lots, scrambled to find any at all. Prices of used cars, trucks and SUVs increased nearly as much as housing.

On February 24, the Russian Federation invaded Ukraine. Since 2014, both had been at war with each other, sort of. Ukraine had gained independence from the defunct Soviet Union, along with the other 14 former "republics" of the USSR in 1992. In 2014 Russia bloodlessly seized Crimea from Ukraine. Embolden by that easy success, Russian Federation President Vladimir Putin looked for more. In the mostly Russian ethnic parts of eastern Ukraine "separatist" movements, given Federation weaponry, declared themselves free of Kiev.

Putin was a former Lt. Colonel in the KGB. As a young man in his 30's, he had been the chief Soviet liaison officer to the East German Stasi, its secret police. East Germany was a communist state on the front lines of the Cold War, pitted against western NATO forces. Putin bitterly regretted the collapse of the USSR and the extension of the NATO alliance into former Warsaw Pact nations and ex-Soviet republics. Putin skillfully reasserted indirect control by Moscow over most of the ex-USSR. Ukraine was by far the richest, the most industrialized and populous. Russia and the United States had feuded since 2014. US Secretary of State Hillary Clinton was loathed by Putin. Wouldn't the election of Donald Trump, who had many business connections to Russia, be preferred to that of Mrs. Clinton? How much, if any, covert help Putin gave Trump in the 2016 is still debated. But once in office after the US election, both presidents formed a friendly relationship.

Putin continued his proxy assault on Ukraine but did nothing else to cause difficulties with the US. Trump's defeat in 2020 seemed to have changed his thinking. There seemed little to lose from a full-fledged Russian invasion, as a new foe Joe Biden was now in the White House. Putin's military and intelligence experts assured him that Kiev and Kharkov would fall quickly. A puppet regime, under Moscow's control could then be installed.

If the US or other NATO countries took any actions, which was doubtful, they would be too little and too late. Most likely there would be a few toothless sanctions enacted again, as the West had imposed in 2014 after the annexation of Crimea.

The February 24, 2022, invasion did not go according to plan. Neither Kiev nor Kharkov was taken. Russian losses in men and material were great. The Ukrainians fought well and exposed the much larger Russian forces as poorly led both strategically and tactically. The US, the UK and most other NATO countries responded by giving Ukraine billions of dollars in weaponry and other forms of aid. A major war casualty was the pump price of gasoline. In the US, they were up nearly 50% in less than six months.

By mid-spring, pundits expected that a GOP "wave election" would take both the Senate and the House from the Democrats. A troubled economy and a President viewed as either ineffective or wrong-headed were the clear catalysts. But in May anonymous information, apparently leaked from the Supreme Court, said that the justices were planning to overturn the 1973 Roe v. Wade ruling. For nearly 50 years abortion had been legal throughout the country. That was a dramatic reversal from just a few years beforehand when it was prohibited in all but a few states. In 1992 the Planned Parenthood v. Casey decision allowed individual states to regulate some aspects of abortion, before protected under Roe v. Wade.

States, mostly in the South, began requiring abortion providers to meet stringent medical guidelines which put most of them out of business. There were some states where only one or two clinics survived. In 2018 Mississippi passed a law which banned most abortions after 15 weeks of pregnancy. That bill seemed to conflict with the 24-week federal standard. After several lower court rulings, the case went to the US Supreme Court. By a six to three vote, the Court decided that the Mississippi law could stand. Five of the Justices (all Republicans and three appointed by Trump) said that abortion is not a federally protected constitutional right. In the aftermath, the floodgates were opened and near total abortion bans were passed in other states.

While horrifying pro-choice Democrats, it was a gift to the party politically. The Dobbs ruling was unpopular with most voters, not just Democrats. While Trump was gone, his Supreme Court clearly was not. Democratic leaders empathically told voters that the Court ruling was ripping the country apart. An unelected Supreme Court would now make decisions that women should make on their own. In summer special elections Democratic candidates for the US House ran better than expected, exceeding Biden's 2020 vote share in all four contests, even winning Alaska's at large seat, Republican since 1973. These results were widely interpreted as a rebuke of the Dobbs decision. Might 2022 be an off-year election like 1962 or 2002, where an unforeseen event helped the President's party keep or gain power in Congress?

Donald Trump left the White House surly and sullen, just before the inauguration of Joe Biden on January 20, 2021. In departing Trump took a large, but unknown number of boxes with him. What did they contain? The National Archives and Records Administration (NARA) wanted to know. Alerted by the absence of several important documents, the NARA contacted the former President's representatives. In January 2022, NARA retrieved 15 boxes of materials from Mar-a-Lago which should, they said, have been kept by the government. But many key documents, including those marked "Classified", "Secret" and "Top Secret" were still missing. Never receiving them back, the Department of Justice issued a subpoena to enforce their return. There was no compliance on the ex-President's part. The FBI raided Mar-a-Lago on August 8, 2022, searching the property and Trump's private office. They found more than 13,000 government documents had remained, of which 103 were considered classified.

Republicans were livid. Yet again the "deep state" was at work! It was spearheaded by an FBI which had been at Trump's throat since the Congressional hearings on alleged 2016 Russian election interference. Releasing the seized documents, to determine any possible legal action for violation of the World War I Espionage Act, was contested by Trump's lawyers. By the end of 2022, nothing had been resolved. Could Donald J. Trump be put on trial and convicted? Can a convicted felon become president of the United States? Would Trump's election in 2024 prevent his possible imprisonment, or literally get him out of jail?

On January 6, 2021, most Republican senators, including GOP leader Mitch McConnell voted to certify Biden as the winner. Trump found that disloyal. Nonetheless, McConnell continued to say that Biden had won fairly and squarely. Both had feuded during Trump's presidency. Donald Trump needed absolute loyalists if he were to become president again, not career politicians like McConnell who put their own interests before his. Trump persuaded most GOP voters that he had won the 2020 election. Only "Democrat" vote fraud had stolen it.

A cavalcade of supplicants went to Mar-a-Lago, hoping to be granted Trump's blessing for their 2022 GOP primary bids. All were required to pledge absolute fealty and to concur that yes, the 2020 election was stolen. After the proper obeisance, some were endorsed, and some were not. Almost every GOP House member who voted to certify Biden was either defeated by a Trump "election denier" in the primaries or decided not to seek another term. The most prominent loser was Liz Cheney, daughter of former Vice-President Dick Cheney and chairwoman of the GOP House Conference. Ms. Cheney compounded her apostasy by serving on the Democratic run "January 6, 2021" House committee hearings, which Republicans declared to be a witch hunt. Cheney soon lost her leadership position and later the Republican primary for her seat in Wyoming.

Candidate quality issues were on the mind of Senator McConnell when asked late in the 2022 campaign about the GOP's chances of retaking the chamber. McConnell did not name names but appeared to be pointing his thumb down at four Republican nominees. Each one had Trump's blessing which had greatly helped him to gain nomination: Blake Masters (AZ), Herschel Walker (GA), J. D. Vance (OH) and Mehmet Oz (PA). None had been a candidate previously for any elective office. The outcome of those four contests would probably decide control of the next Senate. McConnell's comment suggested that Republicans would have done better with other picks. Those should have been candidates who had run and won races before. Candidates that carried less personal baggage, referring to Oz and Walker, could be helpful too.

Not only was the Senate at stake in 2022, but the House as well. Democrats had a tiny majority after the 2020 election, surprisingly having lost 12 seats in the previous cycle. A GOP gain of only five seats would give them a majority. Every ten years the US Census reallocates Congressional representation between states. The Census 2020 shifted just seven seats, the fewest in history. Within each state, districts must be redrawn to reflect changes in population and be approximately equal in size. For a time, it appeared that redistricting would be a wash, and neither party would gain or lose. But New York's Democratic gerrymander was thrown out in state court and Governor Ron DeSantis obtained a highly partisan Republican remap in Florida. The overall advantage was now to the GOP. Yet after all district lines were set for the 2022 election, Biden had won 226 in 2020 to Trump's 209.

Another lightening rod was struck twice by deadly mass shootings in Texas and Illinois. As with earlier slaughters in Connecticut and Nevada, the shooters had used semi-automatic military assault type rifles to commit their murders. GOP leaders offered thoughts and prayers for the victims, reiterating the mantra that people kill people, not guns. Democrats said that without the legal sale of semi-automatic weapons, none of this could have happened. Many called for a nationwide ban on the purchase of assault rifles. Republicans did not agree. A few suggested that tighter background checks on prospective buyers might, however, limit future killings.

Stirred from its slumber by the highest inflation rate since the early 1980s the Federal Reserve began to alter course. In all the 2022 Fed meetings, bank borrowing costs were raised. The Fed's stated goal was to cool-off inflation. The immediate effect was to raise the price of home mortgages and consumer purchases on credit. The Fed's unstated goal was to cool off the demand for labor and increase unemployment. Would it all end a recession? If so, how bad, and long would it be?

Joe Biden's "Build Back Better" infrastructure plan was finally enacted in a modified, much less expensive form than first proposed. Now called the "Inflation Reduction Act" it was last pillar of the Democratic plan to revive the economy and make America fairer and "greener." The August bill included almost none of the tax increases on corporations that it originally envisioned. Most of the benefits helped people who would purchase electric vehicles and make their homes more energy efficient. Companies that develop wind and solar energy were given future tax credits.

Other provisions included capping out-of-pocket Medicare costs and extending Obamacare subsidies set to end after 2022. The chronically underfunded IRS was given an additional $80 billion to add staff and modernize computer systems. Republicans were mortified and claimed the government would now be auditing everyone, not just Donald Trump.

Among Joe Biden's 2020 campaign promises was $10,000 per student loan debt relief. Next to home mortgages, these loans are the single largest component of personal debt, greater even than credit card and auto loans. The cost of higher education had skyrocketed since 1980, roughly doubling in real (inflation adjusted) dollars. Yet the future income value of a four-year college degree hadn't grown by nearly that much. Critics have said that most of the extra tuition costs burdening today's student borrowers have come from institutions adding unneeded overhead and paying insane prices for non-academic help. For most larger universities, the highest paid employees are in the men's football and basketball coaching staffs, not in professorships.

By executive order, Joe Biden fulfilled his pledge. As an extra bonus, he increased the amount for Pell grant recipients to $20,000 per student. Financial analysts expect the forgiveness programs to cost $600 billion to $1 trillion over the next ten years. Many, not just Republicans, argued that Biden's order was unfair to students who had paid their loans. They said Biden's decree would only encourage more students to enroll in programs with little prospects of well-paying careers. And what about those who hadn't taken out loans or gone to college? They were the biggest losers of all. Numerous lawsuits emerged challenging the order's legality, saying that Congressional approval was necessary.

The major parties' campaign messages in 2022 were simple. It's all about abortion rights asserted the Democrats, occasionally adding the existential threat to democracy posed by the GOP and the lurking specter of Trump.

Republicans asked voters: Have you had enough of cascading crime, inflation, and illegal immigration? If so, return a GOP majority to Congress. Stop Biden, Pelosi, and Schumer from further ruining America.

Pre-election forecasts for control of the House uniformly favored the Republicans. The Senate was rated as either a toss-up or slightly tilting to the GOP. After Election Day, only one Senate seat changed hands, with Pennsylvania replacing a retiring Republican with a Democrat. There was a race still undecided in Georgia, where no candidate obtained 50% of the vote, plus one.

There was a moderate swing from 2020 in the House vote. Republicans won 51.7% of the major two-party vote in 2022 after losing by two percentage points in the last election. Turnout declined disproportionately in big city Democratic strongholds such as Philadelphia, Chicago among many others. In the end Republicans controlled the House with 222 seats vs. 213 for the Democrats. In 2016, with a smaller 1.1% margin, Republicans took 241 seats. Remarkably the Democrats fared much better in seats won than voting results in recent cycles would have indicated.

On December 6, 2022, the final Senate race was decided, as Trump primary backed Herschel Walker failed in a run-off to beat incumbent Georgia Democrat Raphael Warnock. What more proof could be asked for, said the GOP establishment, that Trump was now voter poison? Just nominate anyone else and Republicans will win the presidency in 2024!

# 2024 GOP NOMINEE

Will the Republican 2024 nominee be Donald Trump or someone else? Polls now suggest that most GOP voters would prefer it not to be Trump. The conservative pundit class certainly would not, blaming him for the Republican failure to retake the Senate in 2022. Even if challenged by plausible contenders with money and name recognition, Trump would still be more likely to win than anyone else.

On the stump during the 2022 campaign Trump was cagey, only saying he would arrive at his decision "soon." Soon came on November 15, 2022, when he declared his candidacy.

Why did Trump choose to run?

- Belief that he would be re-elected, avenging the 2020 "stolen election."
- Failure of the Biden administration to "keep America great."
- The opportunity to further retaliate against his enemies in 2025 and after.
- Legal difficulties, including indictments and possible convictions. Could a major party presidential nominee be indicted, tried, or imprisoned? There were some indications, in court rulings during Trump's first term, that the answer would be no. Could serving as president be a "get out of jail free card?"

Naturally, all would be out of Trump's control if he were to pass away before the GOP convention, or after his nomination. The status of his health is a closely guarded secret.

# USA 2025

Who are other possible 2024 GOP presidential nominees and what are their chances, should Trump lose in the primaries or stand down before because of health reasons?

- Nikki Haley (SC): A former SC governor and United Nations ambassador, she is well-spoken, a woman of color (East Indian heritage) and is considered moderate by GOP standards. Odds: 5%

- Tim Scott (SC) Senator: The only Black senator now serving, Scott is an orthodox Republican. He is conservative both economically and culturally. Except for his color, Scott is little different from his GOP senate colleagues. Odds: 5%

- Kristi Noem (SD) Governor: Known as a pro-life champion and was firmly anti-COVID-19 restrictions. If Nikki Haley were not in the race, Noem's chances would be boosted. Odds: 5%

- Tom Cotton (AR) Senator: The so-called "Senator from Walmart" is very bright, very right wing and very ambitious. But Cotton has few discernable differences from others who share the same profile. Odds: 5%

- Chris Sununu (NH) Governor: Very popular in a purple state, he was an easy reelection winner in 2022. Sununu could fill the "sensible conservative" lane in the primaries. Odds: 10%

- Mike Pompeo (KS): A former governor, he has good name recognition from his years in the Trump administration. Pompeo took a mini swipe at Trump after the 2022 election, saying "he was tired of losing." Formerly obese, Pompeo lost a reported 90 lbs. to enhance his visuals. Odds: 10%

- Mike Pence (IN) former Vice-President: In 2016 Senator Pence was chosen by Trump as ballast to reassure the GOP's Evangelical Christian voters. He proved to be a reliable but unexciting choice. Pence failed the big test on January 6, 2021, by not blocking Biden's certification as president. Odds: 10%

- Marco Rubio (FL) Senator: Youngish looking and a good speaker in both English and Spanish, he seems more moderate than he really is. At one time Rubio supported Obama's "Path to Citizenship" of which his opponents surely would remind Republican primary voters. Odds: 10%

- Glenn Youngkin (VA) Governor: Elected in 2021, he won in a Democratic leaning state. Youngkin reportedly has his eyes on the prize and has been talked up by the national media. Odds: 10%

- Ron DeSantis (FL) Governor: He was a big re-election winner in 2022. A clever political operator, DeSantis is widely touted as the most formidable Trump opponent should he run. Odds: 25%

- "The Field" (all states): Another dozen or so candidates might join an open race, but few, if any, would last until the early primaries or caucuses. Odds: 5%

# 2024 DEMOCRATIC NOMINEE

President Joe Biden will turn 82 before the November 2024 election. He would likelier than not face a 76-year-old Donald Trump as the Republican nominee. In any previous epoch, a battle of such oldsters would have been thought inconceivable. Has the USA turned into a gerontocracy?

Will Biden run again? Unless health problems (or death) prevent him, he probably will. Biden has devoted his entire adult life to politics. Biden fears the election of Trump, or that of almost any other Republican would genuinely threaten democracy in the nation.

But there are caveats in addition to health issues, which may alter his decision. Biden's approval ratings are low and his chances of defeating Trump, or any other GOP nominee, currently are only 50-50. If impeached by the House, the nation in recession, and his popularity plummeting, Biden may decide that it's time to head back to Delaware or perhaps to somewhere warmer.

If he runs in 2024, would Biden be seriously challenged in the 2024 Democratic primary? That appears unlikely. In 2020 Biden campaigned as a centrist, projecting himself as the only Democrat who could beat Trump. Since the 2020 election, he has moved left with the rest of his party. It would be difficult for any progressive Democratic opponent seriously to complain about Biden and get much traction.

The last incumbent Democratic President to face a difficult primary challenge was Jimmy Carter in 1980. Carter had come out of the blue to become the 1976 nominee and then to defeat President Gerald Ford in November. Carter governed as centrist, much to the dismay of the very liberal Senator Edward Kennedy (MA). Ted Kennedy failed to beat Carter, despite his own fame and Carter's low poll ratings. Underwater in overall popularity, neither Bill Clinton (1996), nor Barack Obama (2012) were challenged in the primaries for reelection.

But if Joe Biden does not run, but remains as President through 2024, who might the Democrats select? Listed below are the contenders and their odds of winning the nomination:

Kamala Harris (CA) Vice-President: As a senator Harris ran briefly in the 2020 Democratic primary contest but didn't last long. Her most remembered 2020 debate moment was taking Biden to task over a 1970s anti-school busing bill which he had supported. Still, she checked off the two most important boxes, female and minority, the Democratic base. With those qualifications she was selected by Biden as his running mate. Odds: 50%

Pete Buttigieg (IN) US Secretary of Transportation: Mayor of South Bend, Indiana for eight years, Buttigieg ran well in the early 2020 presidential contests. He is very articulate, very bright, and seemingly moderate. Buttigieg is also openly gay and married with a husband. Odds: 15%.

Gavin Newsome (CA) Governor: A long-time politico since 1996, Newsome beat back a Republican sponsored recall challenge in 2021, one of the Democrats' few bright spots that year. A progressive, he is nationally prominent and governs the largest state in the US with the most delegates to the 2024 convention. Odds: 10%.

Amy Klobuchar (MN) Senator: As a moderate running in the Democratic 2020 primaries and caucuses, she performed respectably. Odds: 5%

Gretchen Whitmer (MI) Governor: She was rumored in 2020 as a possible Biden Vice-Presidential choice. Since 2021 Whitmer, a moderate, has been Vice-Chair of the Democratic National Committee and easily won reelection in 2022 against Trump-backed Tudor Dixon. Odds: 5%

Bernie Sanders (VT) Senator: He ran in 2016 and 2020, finishing second both times. He will be 83 in 2024. But Sanders is probably through with his own electioneering. Odds: 5%.

J. B. Pritzker (IL) Governor. A billionaire, he won re-election in 2022, albeit by a smaller margin than in 2018. A solid progressive, Pritzker seems to have national ambitions. He used his personal money liberally to win his Illinois races. He could do so again in a presidential bid. Odds: 5%.

"The Field" (all states): Other candidates who may emerge probably are sitting senators, governors, or mayors. Odds: 5%.

Should Joe Biden leave office in 2023 or 2024, and Kamala Harris were to become president, her chances would rise to 80% or greater.

# 2024 THIRD PARTIES

Democrats and Republicans won't be alone on the voters' ballots in 2024. The Libertarian and Green Parties will there be as well, along with many others. What impact will they have on the results? In 2020 all minor parties drew 1.8% of the vote, down considerably from 5.7% four years before.

Non-major parties have fared best in recent elections when one or both major parties' candidates are viewed unfavorably. That happened in 2016 with Donald Trump and Hillary Clinton. Sections of both major parties had considerable distaste for their nominees. Independents had even more. Trump won despite Gary Johnson (Libertarian) apparently taking many more votes from him than did Jill Stein (Green) from Clinton.

In 2000, Ralph Nader ran as the Green Party candidate, a progressive/leftist and critic of Bill Clinton and Al Gore. He won 2.7% of the national vote. The ballots Nader received in Florida almost certainly kept Gore from the White House.

What are prospects for minor parties in 2024? If the election is a repeat of Biden versus Trump 2020, they are probably good. Most voters don't want either to be president again.

In 1992 Ross Perot almost cashed in with a similar dissatisfaction: George H.W. Bush versus Bill Clinton. Perot won 18.9% of the non-major party vote, the highest since Robert LaFollette's Progressive Party bid in 1924. Charismatic, well known and a very successful entrepreneur, Perot led in the polls as the Reform Party candidate in the spring of 1992. Then he mysteriously dropped out of the contest, apparently endorsing Clinton. Perot reconsidered and reentered the race in time for the fall presidential debates. On election day, a plurality of voters said they would have chosen Perot if they believed that he could win.

Is there another Perot-style independent on the horizon in 2024? Results like his would take at least five elements:

1. Money and lots of it, $50,000,000+ just for starters. To run a full race through November, $250,000,000+. Few Cable TV networks are likely to give any independent candidate the free publicity they gave to Donald Trump in 2015-16.

2. Fame

3. Charisma

4. A compelling message, telling why he or she is better than the Democratic or Republican alternatives.

5. A willingness to take the heat. American politics at the highest level is a very nasty full-contact affair, exposing every aspect of one's past personal and financial life. Most non-career politicians are unused to that glare and would not submit themselves to it, at least not for long.

Another third-party candidacy has been suggested, that of Donald Trump, should he lose the 2024 GOP nomination. The last candidate doing so was John B. Anderson in 1980. He had finished behind Ronald Reagan and George H. W. Bush in the Republican primaries but then garnered 6.6% of the general election vote as an independent candidate.

If Trump were to run as a third-party candidate, the result would almost surely be the election of Joe Biden or any other Democrat. But would he? Given the very, very long odds of winning, he probably would not. Presidential races are expensive and getting on most state's ballot is lengthy and costly. Couldn't that time and money, in Trump's eyes, be better devoted to his on-going legal battles? Failing to win would brand him as a three-time loser, once in 2020 and twice in 2024. Embarrassingly, he could be the 21st century's version of William Jennings Bryan.

# TRUMP 2.0?

Inaugurated in 2017, Donald J. Trump entered a new world of incredible power as its mightiest leader. He also experienced unprecedented restraint which he had never known as CEO of the Trump Organization. In place of his company was the government, not only in Washington, DC, but in each of the 50 states. He was constrained by Congress, the Supreme Court, federal agencies and handicapped by his unfamiliarity with what he could or could not do as president.

Trump gradually learned, but not quickly enough. His failed reelection bid had much more to do with COVID-19 and his perceived mishandling of it, rather than alleged voter fraud, or the "disloyalty" of Mike Pence and Mitch McConnell. Should Trump be the 2024 GOP nominee and general election winner, he probably will correct his first terms errors and not repeat them.

Despite his detractors, Trump is intelligent and unquestionably street smart. To enjoy, rather than struggle in a second term, he would press the agenda this book suggests. In doing so, Trump would become a real CEO again, this time of the USA, as a top-down, authoritarian style leader.

Most US citizens work for authoritarian style businesses. Many Americans are worshipers in authoritarian style religions. Would an authoritarian style of government upset many (either on the left or right), if it were sympathetic to their wishes?

What kind of strongman might Trump resemble? Many have suggested some archetypes, including populists Adolf Hitler, Benito Mussolini, Silvio Berlusconi and Huey Long. The first two operated in countries which were converted from democratic republics to one-party (and one man) ruled dictatorships. The latter two were politicians in nations which remained democratic.

Adolf Hitler: The "Great Dictator" held office as Reich's Chancellor and Fuehrer of Germany from 1933 to 1945. He was a professional politician from 1919 onwards and had never held steady employment aside from his service in the WWI era German Army (1914-19). Hitler was of a lower-middle class background and not money driven, but power driven. Hitler was an opportunist, like Trump, but also an extreme ideologue, unlike Trump. Hitler strove: 1. to make Germany the most powerful nation again in Europe after its defeat in WWI, 2. to rid Germany and later all of Europe, of Jews, and 3. to destroy communism in Germany and later throughout the continent. For years Hitler was phenomenally successful and remained popular in the Reich throughout his reign. Two unforced errors in 1941, invading the Soviet Union and declaring war on the USA, led to his downfall.

Benito Mussolini: "Il Duce" was a professional journalist and the leading left-wing Italian Socialist before 1915. His decision to support Italy's entrance into WWI, on the side of the Entente (Britain, France, and Russia), resulted in his expulsion from the Socialist Party. In 1919 he founded the Fascist Party. In 1922, Mussolini instigated a failed coup to overthrow the legal government. Yet, he was appointed Prime Minister by Italy's timid King Victor Emmanule, despite little popular support for fascism. Mussolini came from a middle-class, but radical, landowning family. Like Hitler he had considerable talent as a propagandist and orator. Unlike Hitler, he was obsessed by the need to present himself as an all-knowing and all-controlling leader – a man who never slept. That conceit led to appointing himself "Comando Supremo" of the Italian military, and to make war on Britain, France, the Soviet Union, and the USA. His days ended in April 1945, executed by Italian Communist partisans while attempting to flee to neutral Switzerland.

Silvio Berlusconi: A highly successful entrepreneur, he began his rise in the construction business. That provided the funds to start an advertising agency. A little later, Berlusconi founded Italy's first cable television company. Further ventures led to the creation of a media empire. Legal troubles encouraged Berlusconi to enter politics, launching a new political party and his election as an Italian parliamentary deputy. Deputies, not coincidentally, are exempt from arrest. Berlusconi's new party Forza Italia was a huge success, winning more votes than any others. That victory was helped by massive free advertising on his media network. Berlusconi not only won a seat in parliament, but shortly after he became Prime Minister of Italy in 1994. He eventually served five times in that post for various coalition governments. But in recent years, Berlusconi has been out of electoral politics.

Huey Long: A radical Democratic populist from Louisiana, he began running for office at age 26 and was elected to the state railroad commission. A lawyer by training, Huey (as everyone called him) was as much a "political animal" as Hitler or Mussolini. Elected governor in 1928, then US senator in 1930, Huey attracted national attention for his oratory, showmanship, and leftist politics. Attacked by Franklin D. Roosevelt and New Deal apologists (Arthur Schlesinger Jr. among others), Long was assassinated in 1935 shortly before he was expected to begin a third-party bid for president in 1936.

# REVERSING THE 20TH AND 21ST CENTURIES

Most of the Republican Party is at war with the 20th and 21st centuries. They are at war with social and economic changes. They are at war with the laws and court rulings which have enabled them. In 2025 and after, the GOP will have an opportunity to reverse many, if not all.

What will they change, or try to change?

- Voting Rights
- Free Speech: the 1st Amendment
- Gun Rights: the 2nd Amendment
- Women's Rights
- Affirmative Action for Minorities
- LGBTQ Rights
- Labor Union Rights
- Separation between Church and State
- Independence of Federal Agencies
- Environmental, Safety and Health Care Laws

If they succeed, the United States will be transformed, and legally so. This would happen within the framework of the Constitution. No violence, no revolution, no repetition of January 6, 2021, would be needed.

# SENATE FILIBUSTER IS BUSTED

The very peculiar US Senate filibuster rule, once requiring 67 senators (now 60) to unblock legislation, has been modified in recent years. First, Harry Reid (Democratic majority leader) and later Mitch McConnell (Republican majority leader), removed the filibuster for confirmation of federally appointed justices, including Supreme Court nominees.

Before recent decades the filibuster was rarely used. However, it was regularly deployed in the 1960s by segregationist Southern Democrats to stop civil rights legislation. In the 21st century filibusters are now common. They can block every bill which can muster 41 or more votes in opposition, aside from budget reconciliation.

In 2021-22 almost all Democrats pressed Majority leader Chuck Schumer to remove the filister entirely to pass new voting rights and other bills. But, lacking 50 votes (Senators Manchin and Sinema were not in agreement), Schumer never could. Still, Mitch McConnell threatened possible retribution if that happened. McConnell warned that when the GOP regained control of the Senate, he would keep a no filibuster rule (if enacted earlier by the Democrats), then pass any bills the Republican majority wanted.

With a Republican president and control of Congress, Republican rule could be cemented by eliminating the filibuster for *all* bills. It is simple to do, by passing a rule in the Senate that allows bills to be passed by a majority vote. Those could include:

- Allowing Texas to divide itself into four additional states.
- Prohibiting abortion nationally.

- Insuring "election integrity" by passing a federal statute that would provide strict voting rules to which every state would have to comply.

Of the three items above, Mitch McConnell would very likely want each one passed. The first would likely guarantee continued Republican control of the Senate. The second would reflect his own personal beliefs about abortion. The third would gratify a fervent desire of the GOP base to prevent future "election fraud" which they felt cheated Donald Trump out of the presidency in 2020.

But Senator McConnell might not agree. He might wish to keep the 60-vote filibuster rule, apart from court confirmations. However, given likely pressure by members of his own caucus (including potential rivals for his job) and a Republican president, he probably would yield.

If McConnell were to resist, might he be overthrown and replaced by another Republican senator? Yes. If he were replaced, who would be the probable successors?

- John Thune (SD) is the GOP whip and drew the wrath of Donald Trump when he voted to certify Joe Biden's election in 2021. Thune is well regarded by his colleagues. He is not likely to initiate a coup to oust Mitch McConnell but might be available if McConnell's support appeared shaky.
- Rick Scott (FL) is a relative newcomer and a former governor who harbors barely concealed ambitions to become President. Other Senate majority leaders have become presidential nominees, most recently Bob Dole in 1996. The post might be a useful steppingstone to add to his national visibility.
- John Cornyn (TX) is part of the GOP leadership team and is a 20-year+ Senate veteran. Also, he is well thought of in the caucus.

A maximalist position would eliminate all filibusters. If Republicans do not expect to lose the majority in the foreseeable future, why wouldn't they?

# NEW HOUSE RULES

How long will Republicans keep control of the US House? In the 2022 election the GOP regained House control, after losing in 2018 and 2020. Are there ways in the future where Republicans can do better, perhaps keeping the House in near perpetuity?

Even when winning a minority of the total vote, Republicans now seem to have a structural advantage versus the Democrats. Fewer GOP votes are "wasted" in districts that are overwhelmingly Republican than the Democrats waste in districts which are overwhelmingly Democratic. This trend accelerated in the last ten years.

- **2012:** Democratic candidates won a majority of the two-party House vote but only 201 seats, or 46.2% of the entire House.
- **2014**: 247 GOP seats (56.8%) and 188 Democratic seats (43.2%). The GOP wins 54.5% of the popular two-party vote versus the Democrats' 45.5% of the popular two-party vote.
- **2016**: 241 GOP seats (54.4%) and 194 Democratic seats (45.6%). The GOP wins 51.9% of the popular two-party vote versus the Democrats' 48.1% of the two-party popular vote.
- **2018**: 200 GOP seats (46.0%) and 235 Democratic seats (54.0%). The GOP wins 45.9% of the popular two-party versus the Democrats' 54.1% of the two-party popular vote.
- **2020**: 213 GOP seats (49.0%) and 222 Democratic seats (51.0%). The GOP wins 48.4% of the popular two-party vote versus the Democrats' 51.6% of the two-party popular vote.

- **2022**: 222 GOP seats (51.0%) and 213 Democratic seats (49.0%). The GOP wins 51.7% of the two-party popular vote versus the Democrats' 48.3% of the two-party popular vote. This was a reversal of the last four cycles, but perhaps is only temporarily.

Prior to the Supreme Court's Baker v. Carr decision, involving the apportionment of legislative districts, there was only one federal regulation concerning the US House. That was in the 1789 US Constitution. It stated that representation would be determined by the decennial census, with at least one member for each state, the rest to be allocated by population. There was a special provision for counting three-fifths of each state's slave population, which ended in 1870 after slavery's abolition. There were no rules on the sizes of districts in each state and who could cast a vote in an election. Individual state laws determined those questions.

Before the Baker decision the size of House districts could vary enormously and often did. In some states there were districts eight or nine times larger than the smallest ones. States usually did not alter Congressional boundaries unless they gained or lost representation. Often a state gaining a seat would simply add an "at large" member district that would be voted on by the entire state. On very rare occasions, when a state's government was politically divided, every Congressional district was voted on at large. That happened in 1932 when Missouri lost three seats and the Democratic legislature could not pass a new map over the Republican governor's veto. By statute, not by a court ruling, those at large districts were outlawed after 1968.

The Baker decision altered the way House districts are drawn. The original ruling only dealt with individual districts in each state, saying they must be "substantially equal in population" to each other. Later, the Supreme Court said the way districts are drawn must also protect the rights of minorities. In practical terms that meant the creation of "super-majority" Black and later Hispanic districts wherever possible. Republican legislatures, especially in the South were eager to comply. They packed Black voters into super-majority seats. The results were more Black Democrats in Congress, but far fewer white Democrats and overall, more Republicans.

There are several intriguing scenarios that might play out in 2025 and after.

- Permit states to have some, or all their representatives serve at large. That should help the GOP since the party controls most governorships and legislatures. If most states were to adopt such a law, Republicans could see a net gain of eight to ten seats based on 2022 election results.

- Draw Congressional districts equal in population but based only on their number of registered voters. That could circumvent the census issue of asking respondents about citizenship. As only Americans citizens who are 18 years and older can be voters, that would be the basis for new districting. One or more Republicans states might pass such a law, surely to be challenged in the courts. The Supreme Court might approve, encouraging more to do so.

- The Supreme Court overturns Baker v. Carr entirely, saying the decision was wrong, like Roe v. Wade, and states should again be permitted to draw Congressional districts without regard to equal population. That determination could help the GOP enormously.

# FIRST AMENDMENT AND FREE SPEECH

Freedom of speech, guaranteed by the 1st Amendment, is a cornerstone of the American Republic. It includes the right of the people to assemble peaceably and liberty of the press. For over 230 years the exact legality of what speech is protected, and what is not, has been contentious.

What does the 1st Amendment protect, might protect, or does not protect?

- Shouting "fire" in crowded movie theater? No.
- Spreading false information? Maybe.
- Calling for the overthrow of the United States government? No.
- Stopping internet sites from censoring, or blocking communication? Maybe.
- Publishing damaging, but true information about a person or entity? Yes.
- Banning pornography? No, except for images or depictions of minors under age 18.
- Banning books, movies, or videos? Not now, but yes in the past and not just for pornographic content.
- Banning information on illegal activities? Maybe. Dissemination of literature on contraception was at one time prohibited.
- Criticism of federal government officials? Maybe. The Alien and Sedition Law of 1798 forbade it. That law was never tested in court before it expired.

- Religious freedom and worship. Maybe. The 1st Amendment forbids the establishment of a state religion, as existed throughout most of Europe until the 20th century. However, what religious practices might be allowed or forbidden, is not entirely clear.

What changes could take place under a Republican White House, Congress, and Supreme Court in 2025 and after?

- Calling for the overthrow of the United States government: The Capitol Hill events of January 6, 2021, might be exonerated as a lawful "petition of grievances."

- Blocking internet platforms from certain individuals, or their expression of controversial opinions might be prohibited. This has a been a complaint of the "alt-right," climate change deniers and 2020 presidential election disputers.

- Liable laws might be changed to prevent any damaging information (true or not) from being disseminated that could harm a person or business entity. In that respect, a new statute might mirror those in the UK, or other nations. This has been a goal of Donald Trump.

- Pornography: The definition of pornography has been fluid. At one time, printing vulgar words or producing nude (and semi-nude) photos were illegal. After court decisions in the late 1960s and early 1970s, almost anything was allowed for a while, including materials that would be held unlawful today. A federal ban is unlikely, but the high Court could rule favorably on state bans. Laws might be passed letting states interdict websites deemed pornographic. Authoritarian countries around the world do so routinely, but usually for political content.

- Sedition: A new federal law could be passed to outlaw criticism of the US President and his or her cabinet. It might be patterned after laws now enforced in Russia. The Supreme Court might rule it constitutional. Should, somehow, a new Democratic president be elected, the Republican Congress could repeal the law before the Democrat's inauguration.

- Religion: There are unlikely to be any changes made by Congress. But conservative states may enact legislation to ban the use of controlled substances in religious ceremonies, peyote for example. Some could even attempt to outlaw Rastafarianism since it promotes the use of marijuana.

# SECOND AMENDMENT AND GUN RIGHTS

Guns laws have been among the biggest divides between conservatives and liberals for 30 years. In 1993 a Democratic Congress passed, and President Bill Clinton signed the "Violent Crime and Law Enforcement Act," the so-called Brady Bill. It required a federal background check and a five-day waiting period to take possession of firearms.

In 1994 another bill became law. The "Public Safety and Recreational Firearms Protection Act" prohibited the production, transfer, or possession of automatic or semi-automatic weapons. The law expired in 2004 and despite attempts to renew it, all have failed.

These 1990s laws alerted opponents with biggest the financial stake (i.e., weapons manufacturers) to the dangers posed by any federal gun regulations. It also worried many individual gun owners about future threats to ownership of any firearms.

Guns have been regulated, in one way or another since the adoption of the Constitution. In the pre-civil war slave states Black bondsmen were not allowed to possess them. In the Wild West, the open carry of handguns was prohibited in frontier towns like Dodge City, Kansas and Tombstone, Arizona.

In 1939 the Supreme Court held that "the Second Amendment guarantees no right to keep and bear a firearm that does not have some reasonable relationship to the preservation or efficiency of a well-regulated militia."

Weaponry was not regulated by federal legislation until 1968. That was after the assassinations of President John F. Kennedy, Martin Luther King Jr., and Senator Robert F. Kennedy, leading to the passage of the "Gun

Control Act." The law prevented the interstate sale of weapons and ammunition. Other provisions denied gun ownership to felons, minors or the mentally ill. The Supreme Court ruled in 1980, as in 1939, that the right to bear arms was not constitutionally guaranteed outside of militias.

With the addition of conservative Supreme Court members, there was a dramatic turn in the 2008 case of the District of Columbia v. Heller. The earlier high court decisions were reversed. The Court ruled that the 2nd Amendment protects the right of individuals to keep and bear arms unconnected to service in the militia. Two years later, the high Court confirmed that the ruling applied everywhere, not just in the District of Columbia.

The Supreme Court is now considering whether state bans can prevent individuals from carrying concealed handguns outside their homes and what restrictions might be reasonable.

In 2025, under a GOP administration the following are likely to be pressed for in Congress:

- Repealing some, or all, of the 1968 Gun Control Act, again allowing for the interstate sale and shipment of guns and ammunition.

- A federal conceal and carry law allowing anyone living in a state where so permitted, to do the same in any other state. For example, if a Texan travelled to Illinois, he or she could carry a concealed weapon there as well. The interstate commerce clause might be used for justification.

- Repeal of the ban on private ownership of fully automatic assault rifles, and perhaps even more powerful weaponry. There could be a reasonable argument to make, based on the 2nd Amendment's meaning. Weapons of the 21st century are, after all, not those of the 18th century. Wouldn't every "militia" need them?

# UNITED STATES OF FIFTY-FOUR STATES?

Since the admissions of Alaska and Hawaii in 1959, no new state has joined the federal union.

Before the 2020 election, there was a "buzz" about the District of Columbia becoming the 51st state. That notion went back to the 1970s. It was revived by the heady prospects of a Democrat in White House and control of the House, and Senate. All would be needed to secure passage. While those did happen, no District of Columbia statehood legislation came forth. Even if it had, somehow evading a GOP Senate filibuster, it would have faced serious constitutional challenges before a Republican Supreme Court.

*At least eight other new states could be admitted, without the constitutional issue raised by the District of Columbia.*

They are:

- Texas #2
- Texas #3
- Texas #4
- Texas #5
- Puerto Rico
- US Virgin Islands
- Guam
- Northern Marianas Islands

If the federal government were totally controlled after the 2024 election by the Republicans, only the four new Texas states would be considered.

New state admissions have often been politically motivated and very divisive. Just before the Civil War, the fate of the Kansas Territory was violently contested between Northern and Southern settlers. Its blocked 1859 admission, as the 16th slave state by House Republicans, fueled the South's secession movement the next year.

In 1861 with the Republicans now in complete power, Kansas was admitted as free state. West Virginia followed, rather irregularly in 1863. Nevada, with a census population of just 6,857, joined only eight days before the November 1864 Presidential election to cast its three electoral votes for Abraham Lincoln. The admission of those states helped to consolidate Republican and unionist ascendancy.

In the hyper-partisan atmosphere of today's politics, what wouldn't the parties do legally to find an advantage? Admitting new states would be especially important to gain, or to keep Senate control.

Aside from the question of admitting the District of Columbia, all prospective new states (shown above) would be qualified by current law. Residents of each are US citizens and would have populations of at least 10,000 people, as required by the last 19th century admissions statute, although the provision was ignored for Nevada in 1864.

Democrats would favor admitting the District of Columbia, Puerto Rico, the US Virgin Islands, Guam, and the Northern Mariana Islands. With their tiny populations, the last three could draw much opposition, and not only from Republicans.

The additions of Texas states #2, #3, #4 and #5, are the most intriguing and the most likely. By terms of its admission in 1845 to the union, Texas can divide itself into five states. Were it to do so, each of the five Texas states would, on average, be roughly equal in population to the other existing states in the US.

What might the political implications be? Rather than just one GOP state of Texas, there might be four Republican states and one Democratic state. GOP senators would rise from two to eight, Democrats from zero to two, netting an additional four Republican senators.

While Texas has trended recently from a "Solid Republican" to a "Republican Favored" status, its margin was nearly 10% greater for Donald Trump versus Joe Biden in 2020 than nationwide. Most importantly, for newly admitted states, there is no equal population requirement for representation in the Senate. California has about 68 times more people than Wyoming, yet both have two Senators.

A Texas GOP legislature could place most of its Democrats in a new state of "Mid-South Texas", including San Antonio, Austin, and perhaps Houston. The remainder of Texas (four states in total), with no strong Democratic areas except for Dallas, and parts of the Rio Grande valley could be drawn to each favor the Republicans. Admitting four new Texas states would only require, by Article IV, Section III of the US Constitution, "consent of the (state) legislature as well as Congress."

How would dividing Texas into five parts play with public opinion and most importantly the Texas state legislature and its governor? There would be pressure from Washington, DC. The Republican President would ask Texas Republicans if they wanted the Democrats to regain Senate control. No, of course not, and the new states could prevent that. "Make Texas five times greater" might be the winning slogan.

Four new states in Texas would mean an additional four governors, eight senators and numerous other new state office holders. Ambitious members of the legislature would be eager to run for the positions. The Texas governor might be the toughest to convince. Advocates of the proposal might find a way. Could a plumb federal appointment be inducement enough?

# GOP'S UNFINISHED BUSINESS

There is much unfinished business from Donald Trump's first term and George W. Bush's second term. The majority of that is in domestic affairs, involving government paid health and retirement benefits: Medicare, Medicaid, the Affordable Health Care Act (a.k.a. Obamacare), and Social Security.

In most years, the largest percentage of budgetary expenditures are transfer payments. The federal government taxes younger workers, then sends that money largely to retirees, in the form of Social Security checks and Medicare reimbursements. If younger workers live long enough, and contribute enough, they will be the future recipients.

The costs of Social Security and Medicare, versus revenues received to support them, have been rising. For decades most Republicans have said they are no longer affordable, not without significant reforms. The Social Security and Medicare programs have costs which taxpayers can see in their paycheck deductions. They also know what beneficiaries receive and what they might get someday as well.

Those programs are unlike Obamacare, or other federal budget items (i.e., defense, foreign aid, etc.), which are paid for from general tax revenues or by "printing" money (i.e., deficit spending). The United States Postal Service is an exception. It must be fully funded, including pension liabilities, or the cost of postage will go up.

Republicans opposed each of these programs when enacted by Congress: Social Security (1935), Medicare (1965) and Obamacare (2010). The Affordable Health Care Act is the newest and is financed differently than the other two. Social Security and Medicare are arguably the two most popular federal programs in the US. How might the GOP alter these programs and sell those changes to the American public?

# SOCIAL SECURITY

Social Security was a key part of President Franklin D. Roosevelt's famous move to the left in 1935. By then America had risen from the trough of the Great Depression. The banking system had been saved and prices in the agricultural sector were going up, not down, as before. The New Deal's W.P.A. (Works Progress Administration) put hundreds of thousands of the unemployed on the Federal payroll. Fewer were in the streets selling apples. Almost no stockbrokers jumped out of windows. Private business hiring was slowly rebounding.

Still, mass poverty haunted the nation. The 1930s elderly were the most vulnerable. Unlike today, most needed the financial support of their children or grandchildren. In 1933-34 two left leaning populist politicians, Senator Huey P. Long (D-LA) and Francis E. Townsend (CA), pressed for government old-age assistance.

President Roosevelt feared the very charismatic, nationally renowned Huey Long. While Senator Long had helped Roosevelt to win the 1932 Democratic nomination, he publicly criticized the administration's economic recovery policies as too timid. In retaliation, Roosevelt went to war with Long, placing the Senator's Louisiana enemies in federally appointed jobs. Long was widely expected to run against Roosevelt in 1936 as a leftist independent, potentially throwing the race to the Republican candidate.

The 1935 Social Security Act was a response to Long and Townsend. It was amended and expanded over the next five decades. Coverage was broadened to include more workers. The amount of income subject to it was gradually raised, as was the taxation percentage. In 1935 no more than $85 per year could be taken by Social Security from an individual's earnings. Adjusting for a more than 20 times increase in the cost of living, that would be $1841 in today's dollars. In 2023, up to $9,932 could be claimed by Social Security on incomes up to $160,200.

In the late 1970s and early 1980s concerns grew about the program. Would it go bust? Too much money was going out and too little was coming in. Most of the "20 or 30 somethings" in that era (2023's Baby Boomers) thought they would collect little or nothing in benefits.

Unlike almost any other federal expenditure, Social Security is funded by dedicated tax monies received, then paid out. That provision was included in the original bill to mollify conservative Democrats worried about the monstrous budget deficits stemming from the many New Deal relief/recovery programs. If Social Security hadn't the funds to pay out what beneficiaries had been promised, their payments had to be reduced. In 1982 it looked like that would happen, and very soon.

The prospect frightened both parties, even the very conservative President Ronald W. Reagan. In 1983 a GOP controlled Senate and Democratic controlled House approved, and the President signed a new amendment to the Act. Those changes saved Social Security from its most immediate problems. Increases in COLA (i.e., cost of living) payments were reduced, and taxes were placed on the benefits of higher income recipients. The retirement age was gradually raised from 65, for those born before 1944, to 67 for those born after 1959.

Still, there were concerns. The biggest problem was that Americans were living too long. Social Security was paying out much more than was originally envisioned. In the 1930s the average lifespan was about 60 years. By 2000 it was 77. Retirees collecting checks for 20 or 30 years were no longer rare.

There were other difficulties. Labor force participation, needed to generate Social Security revenues, after zooming in the 1980s (Baby Boomers and women generally) had levelled off. The overall ratio of active workers to retirees being paid, fell dramatically. The oldest Baby Boomers could cash in starting in 2008.

President George W. Bush proposed a reform in 2005 after his 2004 re-election. Bush suggested that at least part of any individual's contribution to Social Security could be invested in private bond, or stock funds. The value of that person's account might become greater than it would be if left by itself. Or it might become less as its critics – including the AARP – pointed out. Despite the wishes of Wall Street, salivating over the next 401K bonanza, nothing happened. Bush's initiative went nowhere.

Rep. Paul Ryan (R-WI), US House Speaker, took up the reform cause again in 2017-18. In 2011 alarmed at the then stupendous $1 trillion budget deficit, Ryan (then Budget Committee Chairman) called for a balanced budget which would include reductions in entitlement payments, which included Social Security. In 2018, a less sanguine Senate Majority Leader McConnell (R-KY) said he found "no interest" on his side of Capitol Hill. Again, nothing changed.

The Democrats have a different view of Social Security. To "fix" Social Security, and keep it solvent, Democrats have suggested the following:

- Raise the amount of annual income that is subject to taxation.
- Raise the employer (but not employee) contribution beyond 6.2%.
- Further tax the benefits paid to higher income retirees.
- Make "unearned income" (not from employment) subject to Social Security taxes, which could include dividends and capital gains.
- Fund some of Social Security's costs through general tax revenues.

Republicans will probably try again in 2025 to reduce Social Security expenditures. Having failed before, what might they attempt that could pass Congress and be signed into law by a Republican president?

A new wrinkle might be to offer potential beneficiaries a lump sum amount in lieu of drawing future payments monthly. That could be marketed as a way "to make your retirement much more prosperous." The lump sum could be invested in the stock market or in real estate. Both of those sectors have historically high annual rates of return, far beyond the small COLA increases typical of Social Security. Maybe the use of lump sum payments wouldn't be restricted. They could be spent on anything: cars, boats, vacations, betting at casinos, etc. Enjoy the good life oldsters!

Buy-outs have been a successful ploy in the private sector for decades. Employees often (but not always) eagerly accepted them. Naturally the lump sum buy-out would be considerably less than the expected future value to be paid out by Social Security. Finance and real estate would be ecstatic to see that enacted. Almost every economic sector would. Spending by senior citizens, normally the most cautious consumers in America, might even explode.

Less imaginatively, the GOP could revisit the reforms of 1983 and probably will. The "full retirement age" could be raised to 70 versus 67 now. "Early retirement age" might go from 62 to 65. Extra money now received when waiting until age 70 for benefits, could be raised to 73. "Everyone lives longer now" would be the argument.

Those reforms would be sold as "America can't afford to see Social Security go broke and here's what we must do." As in 1983, changes might only apply to those under the age of 40 or 50. Americans 55-years of age and over, the demographic most concerned about Social Security, would be unaffected.

## MEDICARE AND MEDICAID

Medicare and Medicaid are hybrids. Some of their costs are recovered via the combined tax levied on employment income, paid equally by employees and employers. But most of the expense comes from general revenues. That shortfall has been ever-increasing as more Baby Boomers retire.

In fiscal 2021 there was a shortage of nearly $700 billion. In pre COVID-19 times, that would have amounted to over 50% of the Federal budget deficit. Republicans have suggested a maximum $100,000 cap on lifetime benefits to control costs. After exhausting it, individuals would be on their own, having to rely on private insurance, personal savings, or family.

Democrats are aghast at a cap on Medicare benefits. In fact, they propose the opposite: *expand coverage to those under the age of 65.* Moreover, they say, Medicare should pay for dental, hearing, and vision expenses. Perhaps assisted living or nursing home care should be added as well. How would those costs be funded? The usual suspects are to raise taxes on the wealthy (families earning $400,000 plus), on corporations and capital gains. How much in new taxes would be needed isn't entirely clear.

Medicaid began in 1965, the same year as Medicare. Medicaid provides health assistance to people with low incomes, including some non-citizens. Its coverage is broader than Social Security, even paying for nursing home and in-home care services. Medicaid resembles, to some extent, benefits available in western European countries.

The federal government (paying 60% or so) and the states (paying 40% or so), share in the program's cost. The last major expansion of the program was in 2010, with the passage of Obamacare. More people were made eligible and income limits were raised. Most Republican states objected. In an important decision, the Supreme Court later ruled that each state could decide to accept or reject the expansion. As of 2022, only 13 states (9 in the Old Confederacy) were still holdouts.

In 2025 or after, that expansion might be nullified by a repeal of Obamacare. Federally paid costs are rising rapidly. There likely will be action, which at minimum, will return Medicaid to where it was before the Obamacare related expansion.

## OBAMACARE

The Affordable Health Care Act came fully into force in 2014, after the bill's 2010 passage. The main goal was to provide health insurance coverage to individuals and families not protected otherwise. Costs were to be offset by taxes on the wealthy and on medical device manufacturers. It appeared that like Medicare, tax revenues would be inadequate, and the federal government would have to make up for any shortfall.

Obamacare has, in the opinion of its proponents, been a huge success. The previously uninsured population dropped by nearly 50%. Insurance companies were made to accept all applicants regardless of pre-existing health conditions. Young adults, under age 26, could remain on their parents' insurance plan. But everyone had to be insured, the so-called "mandate," or be fined.

Republicans weren't happy. They felt it unnecessarily interfered with the insurance marketplace. Government subsidized exchanges might elbow out private companies, perhaps opening the door for more "socialism" in other areas of medical care. Business owners (a core GOP constituency) were required to offer health insurance under Obamacare if they had 50 or more employees. Many firms that had not offered health insurance felt they couldn't afford it.

The insurance mandate was a particular sore point, and not just among Republicans. President Obama, while pressing for the passage said, "If you like the health plan you have now, you can keep it."

That was not true, as millions of Americans discovered to their dismay. If your health plan did not conform to the minimum coverage and benefits called for by the Act, then you had to get a new one that did. Those new plans often cost families $10,000+ more per year than their old ones had. If you didn't have a conforming policy, a fine would be awaiting.

In 2017 Republicans eliminated the mandate, before trying to finish off the rest of the Act in 2018. In hindsight that was a mistake. With the least popular part of Obamacare gone, the rest looked much better. The pre-existing conditions and young adults' provisions were generally well liked, even by Republican voters. When it appeared that Obamacare might be entirely replaced in 2018, the program suddenly became popular. That metamorphosis may have led GOP Senators Collins and Murkowski to oppose repeal. Senator McCain had another reason to vote no.

What might the GOP do in 2025? It is very likely that Republicans will try to pass another repeal and replace bill. With a comfortable Senate margin, no filibuster and control of the House, there would be little risk of a second failure.

GEOFF LOCANDER

# WOMEN'S ABORTED RIGHTS

The freedoms that women have enjoyed since the 1960s are under threat. Those threats include not only access to abortion, but also to birth control, perhaps even to equal employment. The only constitutional guarantee is the right to vote. Other freedoms were achieved through legislation, or court decisions.

With the Supreme Court having overturned Roe v. Wade, the issue has been returned to the states, where it was before 1973. Republicans who now control the House, are almost all anti-choice. But Joe Biden is still President. Any attempt to pass a federal statute outlawing abortion would be vetoed by Biden in the very unlikely event that a Democratic Senate filibuster would not stop it beforehand.

The GOP position on abortion is not popular. Most Americans favor some form of abortion access. Polls show a large majority of the public supporting it in the first 13 weeks of pregnancy.

Should the Republicans win the trifecta in 2024, Senate Majority Leader McConnell (or his replacement) could bring a national abortion ban to the floor. Presuming the Democrats have 41 votes (with perhaps an ally or two among GOP Senators), the bill would be filibustered, under current rules. But a 2025 Republican Senate operating under new rules, could prevent abortion and perhaps other bills from being filibustered. Just 50 votes could then pass a national ban which a Republican President certainly would sign.

That could be just the start. Most abortions now happen with the use of abortion pills. Those would have to be outlawed as well. The manufacture, sale, and use of them might be classified as a felony, maybe even a capital offense if its use could be linked to an aborted fetus. A new section of the Justice Department could be tasked with enforcement, including finding, and arresting violators. A possible name might be the "Unborn Life Protection Administration" (ULPA).

During Prohibition (1920-33), alcoholic beverages could be consumed, but not made, sold, or transported. In the case of abortion, that could extend to the "end user" as well. The woman who, after all, abetted in a murder. The model likely to be followed would be that of the Drug Enforcement Administration (DEA), which deals primarily with drug smuggling from outside the country and illegal manufacture within it (Fentanyl, LSD, MDMA, Methamphetamines, etc.). The DEA is aided greatly by local police departments' narcotics squads across the nation.

In the event of a national abortion ban, that help would be significantly less. In larger cities, especially outside the South, voters are strongly pro-choice. It is hard to imagine citizens of Boston, New York, or Chicago, funding their city's version of the ULPA. Thousands of federal marshals would be needed. The "Untouchables" of Prohibition fame (Elliott Ness, et al) might be revived nearly one hundred years later.

Still, some pregnant women could travel outside the United States to obtain abortions. In Canada abortion is legal for Americans as well Canadians in each province. In Mexico it is legal in a few states, but not most. A Republican president could press those governments to prohibit Americans from using their abortion facilities. The success of that tactic is doubtful. Anti-US Republicanism is politically popular in both countries. But there are two other, perhaps very fruitful avenues:

- Forbid travel outside the USA for a wide range of "illegal activities," including abortion. There is a precedent: the "Sex Tourism Law" which makes it a federal crime under Title XVIII of the US Code. It is punishable by up to 30 years in prison if going to a foreign country with the intent of having sex with a person under 18 years of age.

- The US Customs card that Americans complete when returning to the US, might ask if the person has obtained an abortion, or engaged in any other illegal acts. If someone has, and indicates so on the Customs card, that person might be arrested. If the card is not completed that individual will not be admitted to the country.

Birth control was once illegal in the United States. Largely under the radar before the overturn of Roe v. Wade, its profile has risen. Contraception might be made illegal again. The federal 1873 Comstock

Act made it an offense to publish or distribute books and pamphlets by US mail which discussed contraception or abortion. That law was replicated in many states. Not until Griswold v. Connecticut in 1965, did the Supreme Court rule that married couples could not be prevented from obtaining birth control products.

Some of the same reasoning that ended Roe v. Wade might be used by the Court to return birth control back to states, or to localities. Would it be hard to imagine some parish in Louisiana, or a county in Mississippi or Alabama prohibiting the sale of contraceptives? IUDs and maybe even condoms could be forbidden, except to married couples. Those laws likely would be upheld by the Supreme Court.

Since the Civil Rights Act of 1964, employment discrimination based on sex (Title VII) is not allowed. Before then employers often advertised jobs based on gender: "Help Wanted Male or Help Wanted Female." The same job at the same company where both sexes worked, women were routinely paid less than their male colleagues, especially married men.

The 1964 Act, and those afterwards are congressional legislation not incorporated as part of the Constitution. During the debate over the 1964 Civil Rights Bill, there were objections concerning government interference with private businesses. Yes, most libertarian-style conservatives said, state governments had no right to segregate public school students by race. But why shouldn't a private business be allowed to choose which customers it served, or which employees it hired?

Those questions could come again before the Supreme Court. Chances are that in some instances at least, the right to discriminate would be upheld. Why can't a bakery refuse to make a wedding cake for a gay or lesbian couple if the owner's anti-homosexual moral beliefs are offended? Why can't a company, whose owner's theology says that a married woman's place is in the home, not hire her?

# LGBTQ RIGHTS OR NO RIGHTS?

As constitutional originalists have noted, there is no mention in the document, or any of its amendments, concerning LGBTQ (lesbian, gay, bisexual, transsexual and queer) rights. States once could and did regulate heterosexual relations as well. For most of the nation's history "sodomy" (defined as oral as well as anal sex) was outlawed, including relations between married couples. A thaw began in 1962 when Illinois adopted the then new "Model Penal Code" and removed consensual sodomy as a crime.

By 2003 most states had repealed laws concerning sexual relations between consenting adults. But some had not. On June 26, 2003, the Supreme Court, in Lawrence v. Texas struck down the state law. It ruled that private sex acts are protected in the Constitution by the "due process clause." All other states followed in repeal.

But could anti-sodomy laws be revived in one form or another? Would a very conservative US Supreme Court uphold them? What exactly is the "due process clause?" Found in the 5th and 14th Amendments, it protects against arbitrary deprivation of "life, liberty or property" by the government *unless authorized by law*. Could states not pass new statutes? The mood of the Supreme Court has changed regarding past precedents, Roe v. Wade being foremost among them.

Same sex marriage laws also might be challenged. Pressed by the GOP controlled Congress, Bill Clinton signed the Defense of Marriage Act in 1996. The Act, among other things, allowed states to deny the recognition of same-sex marriage by other states. However, in 1996 no states had legalized them. The legislation was widely viewed as solving a non-existent problem, just a Republican ploy to raise money from social conservatives.

That non-existent problem became real when Massachusetts passed a law in 2004 which allowed same-sex marriages to be performed in the Commonwealth. At the time, while generally popular in the Bay State, it was not in the United States as a whole. In the 2004 general election the GOP used the specter of gay marriage effectively as a wedge issue to turn out their voters. It worked and helped George W. Bush to win re-election.

But attitudes were rapidly changing. By 2011 overall public opinion turned in favor of same-sex marriage. The Supreme Court in two rulings, United States v. Windsor and Obergefell v. Hodges effectively made gay marriages legal in every state.

In 2025 and after, with an even more conservative Supreme Court, might those rulings be reversed? Yes, but probably by state action, not by Congress. States in the deep South, or elsewhere, could challenge them and enact new prohibitions. Federal courts would have to decide. What would the decisions be? Chances are that statewide bans on gay marriages would be upheld. Perhaps other laws would be passed barring homosexual relations, returning parts of nation to the years before 1962.

# IMMIGRATION AND CITIZENSHIP

"As president, I will build a wall on America's southern border and Mexico will pay for it…" said candidate Donald J. Trump speaking many times in 2016.

As the 45th president, Trump's new wall turned out to be less than expected. Portions of an existing border wall, begun under George W. Bush, were extended by roughly 52 miles. About $3 billion was spent and alas, Mexico paid for none of it. The new wall was in fact a high barred metal fence, easily cut through with power tools available at Home Depot or Menard's. Undocumented immigrants, or migrants, continued to cross-over from the southern border.

Trump's new border plan did have some success in the opinion of his supporters. The profile of the Immigration and Customs Enforcement Agency (ICE) was raised. So was the ghastly fear of detention in one of their facilities. Still the migrants kept coming, most driven by desperate poverty.

Some border walls designed to contain populations have been highly effective. From the early 1950s until 1990, communist East Germany constructed and maintained a barrier between itself and West Germany. Its purpose was to prevent East Germans from fleeing to the West and freedom. Hardly any did. The barrier included an adjacent "death strip" where no East German could traverse. Should someone get there, they would be met by landmines, motion detectors (which triggered automatic weapons fire), guard towers and a real wall, not a fence. The barrier was 962 miles in length (including Berlin) and manned by 47,000 armed troops who were under orders to shoot to kill all trespassers.

Should the US build something like East Germany's barrier, the cost would be over $1 trillion. Nearly 100,000 soldiers or border patrol officers would be needed to man it, given the nearly 2,000-mile-long border with Mexico. Chances are that nothing like that would ever be constructed.

Such a wall would keep migrants from entering the US, at least from the south and on foot. But those aren't the only "illegals" in the United States, nor most of those now entering the country. The majority are of European or Asian origin and arrive in the United States lawfully, usually by air with a valid passport or a visa. But these temporary visitors never return home, and therefore have no legal right to remain in the US.

How many of the undocumented are in the US? Estimates now are circa 11,000,000, with about 40% from the Americas, 35% from Europe and 25% from Asia or Africa. How serious are Republicans about stopping illegal immigration? Would they seek out, arrest, and return those now here unlawfully, not just those entering along the southern border? There are laws now on the books, which are largely unenforced. However, they could be.

Current law requires that each employer provide his or her own Employer Identification Number (EIN) along with the Social Security numbers of each of their employees to the IRS. If there is no valid match (the number doesn't exist, or belongs to someone else), the law asks an employer to take several steps, none of which would immediately terminate the employee. Rarely are employers held to account by the IRS.

Tens of thousands, maybe hundreds of thousands of business entities are owned by undocumented immigrants, some not paying federal taxes. Some of these enterprises are difficult and dangerous to uncover (drug smugglers and other criminals), but most aren't. "Out in the open" businesses which could be violators include restaurants, lawn trimmers, and a variety of other household or personal services. Many advertise on the internet and would be easily investigated. Most are not strictly cash businesses. Records of their activities could be obtained from banks, or credit card services. Possible passport or visa violations could be cross-checked with ICE.

Any actions taken to find them could be funded by fines, or perhaps even bounties. It might cost the federal government very little and even generate rare a profit. If a fine were established for illegal residence in the US, say of $10,000, 50% could go to the government and 50% to the bounty hunter who provides information leading to an arrest. There might be many eager informants, with personal grudges to settle, or greed to satisfy.

Rather than the repellent detention facilities of ICE, no children would be incarcerated. Adults, after paying bail (10% of a possible fine) would be let out. A hearing would be held to establish their legal status. This scheme working out effectively would depend on the cooperation of local law enforcement, rather than hiring thousands of new ICE officers. Unquestionably no Democratic controlled big cities would cooperate. But many of their suburbs would, as would most other jurisdictions, especially in "red state" America.

How many would be caught or deported? Perhaps not a large percentage, given their numbers in the US. But some *would be* caught and expelled. Fewer would enter and stay in the US, especially in GOP dominated areas, where the law would most likely be enforced. Most important are the optics. *Republican voters would feel as if their party was doing something, and it was working!*

Who is, or could be a United States citizen? Current law is established both by a naturalization statute for those foreign born and, up until now, by the 14th Amendment to the Constitution. That amendment was passed and ratified in the Reconstruction Era, to allow Black men (then overwhelmingly Republican) to vote in the former slave states. It provides "All persons born or naturalized in the United States… are citizens of the United States."

The contemporary GOP has objected to the inclusion of children of illegal immigrants as citizens. At the time of the 14th Amendment's passage, there were no federal immigration laws. Republicans have suggested that children born of women in the US illegally should not be granted citizenship.

In 2021 the Biden Administration announced the US Citizenship Act (yet to be passed and very unlikely to be), with very different ideas. The bill would allow all the undocumented (called "Prospective Immigrants") living in the US as of January 1, 2021, to remain along their families. They would be eligible to work, get Social Security cards and travel back in forth between the US and foreign countries.

Republican labeled the proposal as absurd, just a free pass for violators. And no doubt they said, in a few years the Democrats would propose yet another amnesty bill and forgive everyone who came in illegally afterwards.

Couldn't the next GOP administration and Congress in 2025 write a different US Citizenship Act, not granting children of illegal immigrants' automatic citizenship or voting rights? A Republican dominated Supreme Court might hold it lawful and not contradicting the 14th Amendment. In many states felons and ex-felons are given not suffrage. Might not the offspring of lawbreakers also be denied?

# LABOR UNIONS

Who were George Meany, Walter Reuther, and John L. Lewis? For most under age 50, those names are only vaguely familiar, if at all. But at one time these labor union leaders were as famous as entrepreneurs Elon Musk and Jeff Bezos are today. Almost unimaginable now, one-third of America's workforce (outside of agriculture) was unionized in the 1950s.

In mid-20th century America, people wondered each year which of the "Big Three" automobile companies the United Auto Workers would target next. Car buyers might discover the Chevrolet, Ford, or Chrysler they wanted wasn't on any dealer's lot, and wouldn't be, not until the strike was over. Work stoppages in steelmaking, coal-mining and other key industries were common. Unions asked for higher wages, better benefits (pensions, healthcare) and more paid-vacation time.

For more than 30 years most American blue-collar workers scored enormous economic gains. If unionized, unskilled or semi-skilled manual laborers with less than a high school education often earned as much, or more, than better educated workers in white-collar trades. FDR's leftist Vice-President Henry Wallace's *Century of the Common Man* seemed to be coming true in America.

The mass union movement was made possible by the New Deal's Wagner Act of 1935 (a.k.a. National Labor Relations Act). Workers now had the right to organize (i.e., unionize) without employer interference. If successful in an election (i.e., the majority of a company's workers in support), the union would be recognized. It would then negotiate with that employer for the wages and benefits to be paid in a specific contract.

That contract might extend for many years, or it could end a year later. If a new contract wasn't agreed to, unionized workers might go out on strike. Employers were permitted to replace strikers with "scabs," but union picket lines effectively kept most struck companies closed.

But there were dark clouds on the horizon. By the early 1970s America's worldwide manufacturing dominance was over. The World War II shattered economies of Europe and Asia had recovered. Less expensive and better made products flooded American markets, especially from West Germany and Japan. Manufacturing employment began declining as companies closed, reduced their work forces, or shifted product procurement overseas. In 2022, less than 7% of the American privately employed workers were unionized.

But for the union movement there was a tiny silver lining: government workers. While craft and industrial unions declined, jobs in the public sector, especially in states and localities boomed. Today the largest union in the USA is AFSCME, government employees. While the formerly mighty auto, steel and miners' unions are shadows of what they were 50 years ago.

Union membership has been transformed. Once overwhelmingly male and white, it is now mostly female and minority. Not coincidentally, as white men left union jobs, Republicans began receiving more and more of their votes. Unions in general (excluding police and fire) are the GOP's most determined opponents. They expend considerable resources, in people and dollars, to promote a progressive/left agenda in federal, state and local elections. That includes higher taxes on the wealthy and corporations, a $15 per hour federal minimum wage, plus additional spending on social programs.

Republicans would happily reduce organized labor's political influence even further especially at the national level. What actions could they take?

Political Contributions: Through "527" campaign committees, unions donate hundreds of millions of dollars in each election cycle, the vast preponderance to Democrats. To evade the Federal Election Committee's prohibition on political contributions by unions or corporations, "527s" don't directly advocate the election of any specific candidate. But the ads created (TV, radio, print or internet) leave no doubt of who *shouldn't* be elected in each race.

Since the "527" is a tax-exempt entity, established by IRS code, that could be altered by Congress. The key for Republicans would be excluding more "527s" likely to be Democratic supporting, than GOP backing. How? A possible approach might be to mandate that every "527" exclude contributions made by any source (i.e., a union) whose funding comes from dues or fees. The new provision could be defended in the courts as eliminating "coercive contributions" taken from union members, or from any other group with such a membership.

Taft-Hartley Act: In 1946 Republicans won control of Congress for the first time in 16 years. Public disapproval of a huge post-World War II strike wave and high inflation helped the GOP to win. The Taft-Hartley Act (1947) amended the 1935 Wagner Act, restricting wildcat strikes, secondary boycotts, and direct political contributions by labor unions. Most importantly, the revision allowed states to pass "Right to Work" laws. Twenty-seven states had such laws as of 2022. Employees in them can decide whether they wish to join a union and pay dues, or not.

The 2018 Supreme Court decision Janus v. AFSCME extended that right to public service employees, even in states where paying such dues is required. Might Congress modify the Taft-Hartley law to include *all* employees in every state, whether in public or private employment?

Independent Contractors: "Gig" workers don't only drive for Uber or other ride-shares. Many are skilled white-collar professionals. Many "gig" workers prefer the flexibility of being self-employed as independent contractors. Others do so from necessity. Their employers enjoy more hiring freedom and much less expense. Independent contractors aren't guaranteed a minimum wage, overtime, paid vacations, or health benefits. They can be terminated at will. Employers don't pay federal taxes on their earnings, or into state unemployment compensation. Nor, of course, do independent contractors have any group bargaining rights.

Employer savings with only independent contractors versus only employees could be enormous. According to the Bureau of Labor Statistics, employee benefits are an astounding 30.9% of total wage and salary costs. A company with only independent contractors might double or triple its profits! IRS codes determine who is or is not an employee. Those codes can be changed by Congress.

# NATIONAL ELECTION LAW?

The contentious 2020 election was empathically highlighted by President Trump's claim that the Democrats had stolen it from him. While at first hardly believed, even among Republicans, it was later widely accepted by GOP voters. Voter fraud had kept Trump from re-election!

No convincing objective evidence was presented that this was true, despite several Republican led recounts. In the Arizona recount, Biden gained votes. Nonetheless, assertions of fraud went on. What did seem true was that the extraordinary 2020 COVID-19 pandemic led to election rules changes that benefited Democrats far more than Republicans. Innovations included, in some states, mailing of absentee ballots to all voters and allowing mailed-in votes to be counted long after the November 3rd election date.

Had those changes *not* been made, would Trump then have won? Yes, quite possibly.

Republican legislatures in many states responded in 2021-22 by passing new statutes which, in general, impacted voters in minority areas who are most likely to be Democrats. Those new laws have restricted the number of polling places, drop-off balloting and even "voter assistance", by offering water to those standing in line to cast their ballots.

There is no uniform national election law, but there could be. GOP action is constrained by constitutional amendments, which include voting rights for former slaves, women, and those 18 to 20 years old. The Constitution, as adopted in 1789, made no provision for those who have, or did not have suffrage. That was left for the states to decide.

If in the majority, what could the GOP do that would be held as constitutional? While states and localities have jurisdiction over their own elections, the federal government *may have* that power for elections to the House, Senate, and Presidency. In the late 19th century into the early 20th, some states allowed women to vote in certain elections, but not in all. There was separate balloting for different elections.

Couldn't a uniform national law do the same? States which conformed to a federal statute could have a single unified election, those that did not would need two elections. The cost of two elections would be enormous, perhaps enough to push some "blue states" to comply.

What could a federal election law alter?

- The Motor Voter Law: This 1993 legislation, pushed by Congressional Democrats, required that states offer anyone applying for a driver's license the opportunity to register as a voter as well. It is not entirely certain which party a potential repeal would benefit, but most new driver licensees are either young (more Democratic) or new to the state (which could be of either party). In repealing the legislation, the GOP might leave it to each state to make their own choice.

- Same Day Registration: A few states allow this, but most do not. Voters who register on election day are generally in Democratic leaning areas. That could be outlawed.

- Absentee or Mail-in Balloting: This is a tricky issue. Absentee voting, in some states helps Republicans. Florida is a prime example. Any restrictions would have to be carefully worded. But states could be prohibited from the mass-mailing of absentee federal election ballots and counting those received after election day.

- Identification Needed to Register: Some states require state-issued identification. Others do not. New legislation could mandate that all states must do so.

- Provisional Balloting: In many states persons who are not on the list of registered voters, but think they are eligible to cast a ballot, may vote "provisionally." What scant evidence exists, suggests these are more likely to be Democrats than Republicans. New legislation could bar these provisional voters from federal election contests.

- Voting Drop Boxes: A "bête noire" of the Texas GOP, it was eliminated by a law passed in 2021. This is another candidate for federal election exclusion.

Taken total, these new rules might yield a net reduction of 1% to 2% of the Democratic versus Republican vote. In the close 2020 presidential electoral contest these modifications would probably have produced a different winner.

# US DOMESTIC ECONOMY

During the 2016 primary and general election campaigns, Trump was cast as an economic populist, at least by the standards of the 21st century GOP. No, he would not reduce Social Security or Medicare payments, nor raise the ages of eligibility. Those were themes of "fiscally responsible Republicans," concerned about the long-term financial viability of both programs. They had earlier warned of an oncoming wave of inflation, due to huge federal budget deficits. That wave, however, never happened.

Trump promised that the then unpopular Obamacare law of 2010 would be replaced by a better and less expensive healthcare bill, which would protect those Americans without employer sponsored insurance. Thanks to three Republican Senators, the Obamacare repeal failed. The only significant economic legislation that became law in the first Trump Administration was the "The Tax Cuts and Jobs" bill of 2017 which largely benefited corporations and higher income taxpayers.

The expected high-rate inflation of the Obama era, which not materialize, did so in the Biden era of 2021-23. The comparatively modest $1 billion budget deficits of ten years ago, more than doubled. The reason was not hard to find, in the minds of most 2022 voters.

Many said that hasty and ill-considered legislation had infused massive amounts of mostly unneeded cash into the economy. Low wage workers could double or even triple their income by not working. Rents weren't collected, mortgages were not paid, and no one could be foreclosed on or evicted. Student loan payments were suspended. Many states and cities prevented gas and electric companies from shutting off services for non-payment.

Pie in the sky had arrived: free money and hardly any bills to pay!

# USA 2025

The piper wouldn't be paid, until he was. Inflation rose to levels not seen since the early 1980s. Everything was more costly: groceries, gasoline, vehicles (if you could find one) and especially homes: up almost 19% in one year! And yet the Democrats, apparently still living in 2020, pressed for even more social spending. The voters said no and returned the GOP to control of the US House.

What would Donald Trump or another Republican president do in 2025? What Biden administration programs, initiatives or executive orders would be cancelled?

- Suspending student loan collection or forgiving them.
- Any efforts to raise the minimum wage or to expand Medicare coverage.
- No additional infrastructure spending, unless used to complete the Mexican border wall.

New (and some old) GOP initiatives would likely include:

- Repeal of the Estate Tax: Villainized as the "death tax", less than 1% of estates pay it. However, that tiny number impacts the Republican wealthy and mega-wealthy donor base and is a high priority for them and their heirs.
- Capital gains reduction or elimination: Expect that in a bill purporting "to promote economic growth." If eliminated it would be a massive boon to the financial and real estate sectors.
- Personal and corporate income tax rate reductions: Look for another decrease, like the 2017 version.
- Sunset laws contained in the 2017 bill: The 2017 tax cuts are set to begin expiring in 2023. Expect those provisions to be repealed.
- Defense spending increases: Additional recruits might be needed to help man the border wall. Otherwise, the money would go mainly to military contractors developing and producing new weapon systems. They are a major source of GOP campaign contributions.

- Federal Reserve System: Trump focused on nominating governors who would keep interest rates low and the economy growing. He would likely do so again. Another Republican president might be more concerned with inflation, should it stay high and select different governors.

Overall Republicans, largely through tax cuts, probably would keep the economy expanding, but with correspondingly higher deficits and perhaps more inflation. Upper income Americans would benefit the most, with more real estate or stock appreciation, and smaller tax bills. "Income Inequality" as progressives call it, would grow wider.

# USA AND THE WORLD

The election of Donald J. Trump in 2016 upended GOP foreign policy and free trade orthodoxy. The war on terror and "nation-building" policies of George W. Bush were rejected for what some called neo-isolationism. Concern over America's leading geo-political opponent since the late 1940s Russia (formerly the USSR) was ended. It was replaced by the People's Republic of China (PRC). However, the Chinese were seen mainly as an economic, rather than a military threat.

Some suggested that NATO, founded in 1949 and the cornerstone of US/Western European security relations, was now obsolete. European members spent far less on their national defense per capita than did the US. And why were US troops still in Europe, 30 years after the end of the Cold War? The USSR was long gone, and Russia wasn't a threat.

Or maybe it still was.

The Russo-Ukrainian war has changed some minds, but not everyone's in the Republican Party. In April 2022, 60 House GOP members, voted against a pro-NATO resolution to support Ukraine against Russia.

How might foreign policy play out in future GOP administrations? There are two scenarios, depending upon the new president:

- Trump is elected again in 2024, or another candidate is, with a similar foreign policy platform.
- A Republican with a "Bush-like" foreign policy becomes President instead.

Key points of policy differences are:

- Russia/Ukraine: Trump would take a pro-Russian attitude towards the conflict, should it still be going on, and not supply Ukraine with weapons or even humanitarian aid. A Bush style Republican would probably continue the general line of Biden's policies of limited military help to Ukraine with minimal risk of war with Russia.

- China/Taiwan: Trump took no action against China after it ended self-government in Hong Kong and suppressed dissent there. That has emboldened the PRC. With Russian military moves in Ukraine and elsewhere, the temptation has been great to "reunite" Taiwan with China. Russia's difficulties in Ukraine and the vastly troublesome task of crossing the 110-mile Taiwan strait and seizing a nation of 24 million might give the PRC some pause. An enhanced presence near Taiwan of the US Navy, plus more US military aid are the best guarantors that the PRC would not invade. Certainly, a Bush-like GOP president would do that. With Trump, that is not a given.

- North/South Korea: Early in the Trump presidency North Korea seemed to be the flashpoint of a potential war. Employing his well-known dealmaking skills, Trump met and charmed the current ruler of the Kim dynasty into a temporarily more pacific attitude. But North Korean nuclear development has continued, along with menacing missile tests. Either a Trump or a non-Trump administration would likely ignore the Korean peninsula. There are much greater threats posed by China and Russia.

- The NATO Alliance: Trump had many business connections to Russia before his Presidency. Meetings with Vladimir Putin and his representatives were cordial. He imposed none of tariffs against Russian goods that he had on other European nations. If elected in 2024, Trump might effectively end the Alliance by withdrawing US troops from Europe, perhaps even giving-up the use of airfields in Britain. A Bush-like Republican would not. He or she would probably add to US military forces already in

Europe and encourage potentially threatened non-NATO countries to join the Alliance.

- Mexico and other Latin American nations: Little of Trump's border wall with Mexico was built. But a new term for Trump would mean more funding and more resources devoted to border protection. Couldn't many of the 100,000 US military personnel in Europe be re-deployed along the southern border? A Bush-like Republican would pursue border security more vigorously than the Biden Administration has, but with less money and personnel than would Trump.

- The Middle East including Israel, Iran, Saudi Arabia, and all the Gulf States: Both Trump and a non-Trump GOP president would pursue similar policies. Complaints of Saudi human rights oppression and its war in Yemen would be rare, if ever. Under any Republican the chances of a military strike on Iran, perhaps teaming with the Israelis, would rise.

- Trade: Biden kept in place most of Trump's tariff increases. Either Trump or another Republican would no doubt keep them as well, if only for revenue.

# FEDERAL PATRONAGE ARMY

Donald Trump's first administration was plagued by difficulties with federal agencies. Many refused to yield to his demands. Accustomed to the top-down authoritarian structure of the Trump Organization, he was often frustrated by the heads of agencies, often long-time civil servants. Among the reported difficulties were:

- Dr. Anthony Fauci and the Center for Disease Control (CDC) responses to the COVID-19 pandemic.
- U.S. Census Bureau's resistance to proposed new 2020 decennial Census forms asking for information concerning citizenship.
- Environmental Protection Agency (EPA) opposition and foot dragging on GOP sought environmental deregulation initiatives.

These were just some of the federal agency actions which harmed the administration politically. Very unhappy, Trump issued Executive Order 13957 which created a new job classification in October 2020: Schedule F appointments. Employees under it would not be covered by US Civil Service rules and regulations. Promoted as a tool to improve "performance and accountability," the Order was generally viewed as a scheme to bring many more political appointees into federal government positions that in any way "handled policy decisions." Those might include scientists, lawyers, and health officials. Their employment would be determined by the administration then holding office, not by US Civil Service rules.

On January 22, 2021, just two days after his inauguration, Joe Biden issued an executive order rescinding Trump's 2020 order.

Should a Republican president be elected in 2024, Executive Order 13957 would likely be reinstated, perhaps with some modifications to extend the scope of positions covered to include even persons *who do not handle policy decisions.* There is a pervasive GOP fear of the "deep – state." It is the belief that within the federal government there exist networks of entrenched bureaucrats who pursue their own agendas, undermining those of the elected administration.

Employing perhaps thousands of GOP partisans in middle and lower-level federal jobs would create an old fashion spoils system to reward their labors in producing votes or monetary contributions. These new appointees also could keep a watchful eye on the machinations of any deep-state colleagues and report them to the administration.

Modifying, or eliminating the Hatch Act would be another juicy target. The Hatch Act, first passed in 1939 and modified many times since, restricts political activity by federal employees. Together with a renewed, or modified Executive Order 13957, it could provide a federally paid political army to the GOP administration.

# CHURCH AND STATE

The US tax code prohibits religious groups (classified as 501-C organizations) from endorsing or contributing funds to political candidates and causes. Doing so would put their tax-exempt status at risk. But if allowed, they could funnel vast sums of unregulated money into the political arena.

Conservative religious leaders have long complained that the prohibition muzzled the expression of their faith. In February 2017, President Trump committed himself to rescinding the ban, the so-called Johnson Amendment passed in the 1950s. On May 4, 2017, Trump signed an executive order "promoting free speech and religious liberty." It was hoped that the order would soon be codified into law as part of the 2017 tax legislation. However, it was not included. The Senate parliamentarian ruled it not germane to the budget reconciliation bill.

Critics complained that a repeal of the Johnson Amendment would lead to a substantial growth in tax deductible contributions and could corrupt the primary mission of churches, that being the saving of souls. The Roman Catholic Church, with the largest membership in the US, does not permit funds to be spent on political candidates, nor does it offer endorsements. Neither do the Mormons, nor main-line Protestant denominations.

However, white fundamentalist Protestant leaders were strongly in favor of the repeal. In the US, especially the South, their church memberships are made up almost exclusively of Republican supporters.

Given the very high potential of financial benefit to Republican candidates, it is difficult to believe that the GOP would not press for repeal of the Johnson Amendment. That effort would likely occur after the filibuster's complete removal from Senate rules.

# WHO NEEDS PUBLIC EDUCATION?

"Give me the child until he is seven years old, and I will show you the man." The quote is attributed to Ignacio Lopez de Loyola, 16th century founder of the Society of Jesus, the Catholic Jesuits.

The federal government plays an important, although limited part in education. It played almost no role financially except through Land Grant colleges until 1944, when the "G.I. Bill" gave assistance to send millions of WWII veterans to college. Cold War fear of Soviet missile technology and a perceived US lag in science (1957's Sputnik launch) led to the enactment of the National Defense Education Act (NDEA) in 1958. The NDEA provided tens of millions of students with low-cost loans to attend colleges and universities.

Although state and local governments provide over 90% of local school funding, many Republicans are unhappy with public education. They feel the public school system is a progressive/leftist platform to propagandize and mislead the youth in their communities. They also ask: why should my tax dollars be spent on an educational system that my children don't use? If I homeschool, why can't I be compensated like teachers are in public schools?

The GOP could take these complaints and turn them into federal law. Taxpayers whose children were enrolled in private schools could be credited for tuition. If a taxpayer homeschools her or his children, the labor expended could be calculated as a tax credit, or perhaps even as a cash payment.

These laws, if enacted, would provide a significant boost to all religious schools, which are more likely than not to be conservatively inclined.

They would also put money into the pockets of homeschooling parents who are strongly Republican.

The federal government provides money to education at all levels not only through the Department of Education, but also with other programs such "Head Start" (Health and Human Services Department) and "School Lunch" (Department of Agriculture). No doubt, many conservatives would contend, too much money is being spent on them. Couldn't many of those programs' dollars be used instead to provide home-schoolers tax credits or cash? Better yet why not slash all federal aid to education to help balance the budget?

# THE STRANGE DEATH OF DEMOCRATIC AMERICA

Could the Democratic Party soon become irrelevant? Will the party prove incapable of winning future presidential elections or congressional majorities? How close are the Democrats to fracturing and losing significant support?

Since its beginnings in the late 18th century as a small land holders' anti-Federalist party, the Democrats (originally called the Democratic-Republican Party) have undergone several metamorphoses. The dominant New Deal Coalition of the 1930s and 1940s included, in roughly equal parts, Southern whites (some conservative economically, others populist, almost all segregationists) and Northerners, largely pro-Franklin D. Roosevelt economic liberals.

By the mid-20th century there was a growing push for civil rights. It was led by a cohort of younger Black voters who had left their ancestral GOP roots and white Northern progressives. "Feminism" was still almost exclusively a Republican issue. Democrats, including John F. Kennedy, mocked the GOP's interest in "women's equal rights." The "Democracy" (as it was called in the 19th century) should continue as the white working man's party.

That was until 1963-65, when in a veritable revolution, the Democrats shed their allegiance to segregation and to an exclusively white-ruled South. In relatively good order, Democrats survived and made a transformation to the party of civil rights, later of feminism, and much later of gay rights. But will the Democrats survive beyond 2024 as a party which will win national majorities?

The title of this chapter is adapted from George Dangerfield's masterpiece, "The Strange Death of Liberal England." Dangerfield describes how social changes in Britain and the rise of the Labour Party as "the logical left" or progressive alternative, ended the Liberals ability to win general elections in fewer than 20 years. Before World War I Liberals (formerly called Whigs) and Conservatives (Tories) had seesawed in command of the UK Parliament for more than a century.

The same is happening now in the United States. Democratic Socialists (Bernie Sanders, the House "Squad") and their progressive allies will likely dominate Democratic politics at the national level after 2024. Joe Biden is likely the last centrist and last straight white male who will win the Democratic nomination. Despite stronger support from college educated voters, who tend to be economic moderates, the left/progressive wing of the party is in the ascendancy.

Nothing suggests that working class whites will not continue to become more Republican, or that college educated whites, less so. Black voters in general will remain with the Democrats, but perhaps (as in 2022), turning out in fewer numbers as voters. Hispanics are trending towards the GOP, especially among higher income earners. Asians are both better educated and wealthier than most Americans. While mostly Democratic supporters, they are highly sensitive to the issue of crime, which favors the Republicans.

The center is not holding, just attempts in 1860 to keep the Democrats united over slavery failed, they are now failing over economic and cultural issues. Most probably, unhappy middle-of – the – road Democrats, Independents and some Republicans will form a new party. The truncated Democratic Party will continue in a leftwing form, garnering perhaps 40% of the votes. In the foreseeable future, it might never win another presidential election, nor either branch of Congress.

# USA: A FAILED DEMOCRACY?

The last decade of the 20th century witnessed an explosion of democracy. The USSR collapsed and along with it, Soviet satellite regimes from Mongolia to East Germany. Renowned political scientist Francis Fukuyama famously proclaimed that this was "the end of history", nothing would change in the future. Liberal (i.e., market driven versus state socialist driven) economies had prevailed. The West won the Cold War. Peoples throughout former communist nations would adopt democratic style governments, as in Western Europe and North America.

And they did, for a while. But the difficulties of converting state run economies to capitalist ones were enormous. Everywhere unemployment soared. Lifetime savings often became valueless. Ethnic tensions rose, once held in check by centralized police-states. Many newly free citizens unhappily discovered that they were now minority nationalities, subject to governance by hated neighbors they had once dominated.

The end of history ended with bloodbaths in the former Yugoslavia, Chechnya, and elsewhere. In Russia, ex-KGB colonel Vladimir Putin's rise to power concluded a brief experiment in democracy.

Out of the dustbin of history, novel regimes arose in Europe. Two of them – Poland and Hungary – might give us an idea of what the US could look like as a failed democracy.

Poland: The Law and Justice Party was founded by brothers Lech and Jaroslav Kaczynski in 2001. In 2015 the party won a majority of seats in the Sejm (Poland's parliament). Notably the party gained control of the media, restricted freedom of speech and packed the courts with supporters of the Law and Justice Party. It remains in power, reelected in 2019. The party opposes gay rights. Its base of support is in the rural, least prosperous areas of the country, much resembling GOP strongholds in the US.

Hungary: Since 2010 the nation has been governed by the Fidesz-KDNP Alliance. Both parties are nationalist, populist, conservative and anti-immigration. Since 2010 the Alliance has held a super-majority in Hungary's parliament, although only once winning a majority of the popular vote. Notably, the country has not supported Ukraine in its war with Russia, despite an historic enmity last evidenced in 1956 when Soviet troops bloodily crushed Hungarian freedom fighters.

# CIVIL WAR OR SUCCESSION?

"House divided against itself cannot stand," Abraham Lincoln famously said, quoting the Bible. His 1858 Illinois Senatorial debate opponent Democrat Stephen A. Douglas retorted that the United States had in fact stood, "half free and half slave," since its founding.

On January 6, 2021, the Capitol building was besieged and entered by protestors demanding that Joe Biden not be certified by Congress as the next President. It was seemingly America's first insurrection since 1861. Although harrowing, the "rebellion" lasted only a few hours and involved just a few hundred people who stormed the building and breached police barricades.

At first the protesters' actions were generally condemned by both Republicans and Democrats. But familiar partisan divides soon surfaced. Nationwide, most GOP supporters felt that Trump had won the 2020 election, not Biden. Wasn't the Washington, DC protest as legitimate, they said, as the violence and looting in scores of Democratic cities following the death of George Floyd?

Many articles and some books have been written about the potential of a civil war in the United States. The divisions between the Left and Right in American politics are profound, on both economic and social issues. What is potential of a genuine civil war in the United States, or of succession by parts of it?

History has examples of real civil wars, which were often combined with wars for independence, or succession.

- England 1640s Civil War: Combatants were King Charles I against most of the English Parliament. This was in a civil war for control of the country. Attempts were made at compromise, but King Charles I firmly held that his God-given royal prerogatives could not be usurped. They were not, until he was beheaded by order of the Parliament dominated by Oliver Cromwell.

- America 1775-83 War of Independence and Civil War: Combatants were a plurality of rebellious or patriot American colonials versus the British government allied with a smaller number of so-called Tory or loyal colonists. The British government tried to compromise after the 1776 Declaration of Independence, but with effective military aid coming from France, the patriots refused, and Britain agreed to recognize United States sovereignty in 1783.

- US 1861-65 War of Independence and Civil War: Combatants were most of the slave states (seeking independence from the federal union) against all the free states, determined to deny that independence. It was not a war to overthrow one government and replace it entirely with another. The American civil war was a counter-revolution by a smaller part of a nation against its larger part. Only in a few border states, Missouri for example, was there a war between civilian irregulars.

- Ireland 1916-22 War of Independence and Civil War: Combatants were the British government fighting pro-independence Irish irregulars, called Volunteers, and identifying with the Sein Fein Party. The 1916 Easter Rebellion began the conflict which ended, after stops and starts, in 1922 with the partition of the island into the Irish Free State (twenty-six counties) and Northern Ireland (six counties) which remained in the United Kingdom.

- Russia 1918-21 Civil War: Combatants were Bolsheviks and Socialist allies versus Monarchists with middles-class or bourgeois allies. The February 1917 revolution overthrew Romanov Tsar Nicholas II. The October 1917 revolution deposed the monarchy's replacement, the Provisional Government, led by Alexander Kerensky. Following the Bolshevik takeover, anti-Communist officers of the former Imperial Army and Navy fought to end the Leninist regime. They nearly succeeded, but a series of defeats in late 1919 doomed them to failure.

- Spain 1936-39 Civil War: Combatants were pro-Republican leftists including Socialists, Communists and Anarchists against Nationalist rightists including Monarchists, Fascists, and most of the middle-class. Helped enormously by military aid (weapons and troops) from Mussolini and Hitler, the Nationalists, led by General Francisco Franco were victorious. They imposed a rightist authoritarian regime that lasted over 40 years.

Would conditions in the United States of 2025, should Republicans gain power, resemble any of the above? What events could happen, and could they lead to a civil war or to succession?

- Civil Protest: Common throughout American history. Odds: 100%

- Civil Disobedience: Frequent in the 1960s and 1970s with the civil rights movement and Vietnam War protests. Those happened a few times since, as in the lead-up to the 2nd Iraq War. Odds: 95%

- Random Civil Disorder: Rarely has occurred on a regular basis, but the 2020 riots after George Floyd's death are a likely portent of what might take place. Odds: 75%

- Organized Civil Violence: The events of January 6, 2021, at the Capitol Building could be a model. Before then, in the 1960s and 1970s, extreme leftists (Weatherman SDS Faction, Black Panthers and Symbionese Liberation Army) committed many violent acts. Odds: 60%

- Armed Uprising: None have occurred since 1861. Advances in central state controlled military technology (aircraft, tanks, etc.) make warring against the Federal government much less feasible in the 21st century. Odds: 5%

Future violence, organized or at random, could include attacks on GOP associated entities such fundamentalist churches, media outlets (Fox, et al) and personalities, as well as political leaders. Most targeted might be conservative Supreme Court justices, Republican senators, congressmen, and governors.

Should GOP rule be firmly established after the 2026 Congressional election, some strongly Democratic states may decide leaving the federal union is the best and maybe their only option. These states would ask their legislatures to introduce ordinances of succession, as states did in the South (1860-61). If approved by legislatures and voters, they would declare themselves independent, perhaps forming a new confederacy.

While gleefully suppressing breakaway rebel states by using the US military, might the GOP cash-in on another opportunity? In 1863 West Virginia was admitted to the union as a new, loyal state severed from the rest of Confederate Virginia. The same might happen in the future, adding new Republican states broken off from disloyal Democratic ones. Perhaps a dozen or more new GOP senators could join and swell an already strong Senate majority.

# GOP RULE FOREVER?

While seemingly an eternity to the opposition, extended one-party rule in democratic countries is relatively rare. In the United States, the longest period in the past one hundred years was the 14-year Democratic control of the Presidency and both houses of Congress from 1933 to 1947. In the United Kingdom, Conservatives ruled from 1979 to 1997. For quasi-democratic countries, the span has been much longer. In Mexico, the PRI Party reigned from 1929 to 2000. In South Africa, the apartheid National Party did so from 1949 until 1994.

The Republican Party that gains power in 2025 and tries to stay in power afterwards, likely will not reflect America. It will be generally viewed as too socially conservative and regressive economically. GOP rule will be enabled by an Electoral College skewed to their advantage, a Senate even more skewed and a Supreme Court decidedly to the right of public opinion.

While temporary disequilibrium has long been the US political norm, the equilibrium has almost always been reestablished soon fairly to reflect the will of the voters. But what if it is not? Minority rule is common in non-democratic countries today where most people don't vote freely. The world's population living in fully democratic nations is an estimated 6%. The United States is considered a "flawed democracy" according to the Democracy Index.

The GOP will almost certainly do what is necessary to remain in power. The question is not what tools will be used, as those have been outlined in this book. The main question is whether a transition to one-party Republican rule will be soft, hard, or even very hard.

The United States has never been a democracy (meaning the people directly rule) in the way that Athens or other Greek City States once were, or at least seemed to be. Like Athens, the founders of the American Republic did not allow women, nor slaves to vote. At the beginning of the Republic, white men who did not own property could not exercise the franchise in most states.

Over the past 150 years that system evolved to something which we now somewhat misleadingly call democracy. There are no property qualifications, or ones based on race or sex. Usually, the will of the majority does prevail, eventually. But, in a republican system of government, the people rule only through their elected representatives.

This book forecasts that the "democratic republican" system that has held sway in past years will be replaced. What follows in 2025 will be either a velvet glove, or an iron fist in which a minority of Americans will impose their will over the majority.

SOFT TRANISITION: Democrats cooperate with Republicans and self-destruct as a party that can win the Presidency. Only left-wingers are nominated for the top of the ticket in the future. In the Senate, moderate incumbents are defeated for renomination. In turn, disgruntled middle-of-the road Democrats and Independents form a new party which garners a significant percent of the presidential vote. The new party also runs candidates for Congress as well as in state and local elections. Meanwhile, the GOP wins the House, Senate, and Presidency in future cycles. Opposition by progressives and leftists to GOP rule is peaceful and there is no organized political violence.

HARD TRANSISTION: Most Democrat officials in most blue states defy GOP laws on abortion and restrictive national voting rules. Abortion clinics operate openly in most Democratic big cities. Local boards of election in most Democratic states refuse to comply with new federal voting laws. Meanwhile political violence is endemic. Many GOP politicians and those in the conservative media are assaulted. The Supreme Court deliberates only in an undisclosed location.

VERY HARD TRANSISTION: The Republican President declares a national emergency, sending US troops into illegally defiant states. The 19th century Posse Comitatus Act is repealed, allowing the military to intervene. Hundreds of Democratic political leaders are arrested and charged with sedition.

The President replaces "outlaw" Democratic governors with loyal Republican ones. By acts of Congress, ten new US states are created and admitted, cleaving the loyal (i.e., Republican parts) from the disloyal (i.e., Democratic parts). New states include South Illinois, North New York, and East California. With a three-quarters majority of states agreeing (including newly admitted ones), a Constitutional Convention is called.

The new United States Constitution of 2032 is ratified, harkening to the originalist intent of 1789. The president and senators are elected indirectly by state legislatures. Each state determines voter qualifications, within Congressional guidelines. "Seditionist" parties, such the Democrats or Democratic Socialists, are not allowed on the ballot.

# TIMELINE 2023-2027

Below is a timeline of what *may* happen through 2027. A 2024 Biden versus Trump rematch is selected below, with perhaps a 30% probability of taking place. But literally dozens more are possible: Biden versus Ron DeSantis, Kamala Harris versus Trump, etc.

## 2023

EARLY 2023: The US Supreme Court affirms all cases involving state restrictions placed on abortion, including Oklahoma's total ban on the procedure. A GOP House panel probes Hunter Biden and concludes that he should be indicted for criminal behavior. Numerous House investigations into Joe Biden's alleged misconduct are launched. The Republican field of announced or rumored presidential candidates include Donald Trump, Nikki Haley, Ron DeSantis, Chris Sununu, Tim Scott, Greg Youngkin and Larry Hogan. Eighty-year-old President Joe Biden declares his bid for a 2nd term as president.

SUMMER 2023: The prime interest rate continues to rise to levels unseen in 15 years. Housing sales keep declining. Joe Biden's approval rating goes down and stands at 40%. A higher federal debt ceiling is blocked by the House GOP, leading to a government shutdown. During a floor debate on stricter gun laws, a Republican congresswoman waves an AR-15 assault rifle and vows "no one will ever take this away from me!" No new 2024 fiscal year budget is approved. House Republicans demand no increase in federal spending, excepting the military, above 2023 levels.

OCTOBER: Donald Trump selects Congresswoman Elise Stefanik (NY) as his Vice-Presidential running mate. Trump further says that he will not participate in GOP debates during the primaries. Trump claims doing so would only help those "who don't want America to be great again" adding, "there is only one MAGA candidate in the race – me."

NOVEMBER: "Off-off" year elections suggest a GOP trend. Incumbent New Jersey Democratic Governor Phil Murphy is ousted by a Republican, as is Louisiana Governor John Bel Edwards.

DECEMBER: In a non-binding resolution, by voice vote, the House declares that the 2020 Presidential election was likely stolen by the Democrats. The vote is considered a test of orthodoxy to garner Donald Trump's endorsement for any 2024 Republican candidate.

# 2024

JANUARY: Eleven Republican state legislatures pass bills which allow their chambers to certify the winners of all state-wide elections, including those for president and senator, regardless of voting tallies reported by individual counties.

FEBRUARY: In GOP primaries and caucuses Trump wins the most delegates in each state, except New Hampshire, won by its sitting Governor Chris Sununu. Too many anti-Trump Republicans are in the race, says the media. The Ron DeSantis boom is fading fast.

MARCH: On Super Tuesday Ron DeSantis triumphs in Florida and Greg Youngkin wins Virginia. Trump triumphs everywhere else and has a large lead in the overall delegate count.

APRIL: U.S. Commerce Department says unemployment has risen to 5.3%. Inflation is up by over 4% from 2023. Housing sales continue downward. Despite much better availability of the new 2024 vehicle models, auto and light truck sales fall 12% from 2023. New sticker prices are higher, averaging 9% more than 2023 models.

MAY: Except for Chris Sununu, all other GOP candidates have dropped out of the race.

JUNE: Supreme Court decides that individual gun rights cross state lines, as an Arkansas man successfully appeals his conviction for carrying a concealed weapon in California. The case is compared by some to the Court's 1857 Dred Scott decision which involved taking a slave (Scott) into a free territory.

JULY: In Milwaukee, Wisconsin Donald Trump is easily nominated along with Elise Stefanik, his running mate. To avoid "the distortions and lies of the fake news media", Trump says neither he nor Stefanik will debate with Democratic opponents in the fall.

AUGUST: A nearly unopposed Joe Biden is renominated, and Vice-President Kamala Harris is again on the ticket. Biden pledges to push "Medicare for all at age 55", levying a 10% surtax on corporations and high-income earners to pay for it.

SEPTEMBER: A fiscal year 2025 federal budget is passed by Congress and the debt limit is raised. There will be no government shutdown, at least through January 2025.

OCTOBER: Donald Trump and Joe Biden are neck and neck in the polls. Libertarian and Green parties show surprising strength and could garner nearly 10% of the vote according to some prognosticators, a signal that many Americans are unhappy with the two major party candidates.

NOVEMBER: Biden wins the popular vote by 48% to 47% for Trump. But Biden loses the electoral vote as Trump flips Arizona, Georgia, Michigan, New Hampshire, Nevada, Pennsylvania, and Wisconsin. Republicans gain new five Senate seats, losing none, and thus control the chamber. In the House the GOP nets six additional seats. Eligible voter turnout is lower. In 2020 an estimated 67% of those who could cast ballots did so, but only 62% in 2024. Minority and younger voters have the greatest falloffs.

DECEMBER: Having lost Senate control, Chuck Schumer is challenged by Elizabeth Warren for the position of Senate Minority Leader. Schumer keeps his post, reportedly by 27 votes to Warren's 19.

# 2025

JANUARY: Despite a 54 to 46 advantage over the Democrats (the biggest margin for either party since 2013-14), two GOP senators Susan Collins (ME) and Lisa Murkowski (AK) are uncertain votes concerning abortion and perhaps other issues. Majority Leader Mitch McConnell (who will retire in 2026), agrees that there will no filibusters for any legislation in the new Congress. Threats of a challenge to his leadership are rumored as one reason for his decision.

In the January 20, 2025, inaugural address Donald Trump decries the shameful conditions in the country which were caused by Joe Biden and the Democrats: recession, inflation, crime, and huge deficits. Citing "an historic landslide victory", Trump vows his new administration will make Americans "feel great again about America."

FEBRUARY: The administration removes all sanctions against Russia and announces that most US troops stationed in Europe will be transferred back to the US. Congress appropriates $50 billion for border security, including funds to complete the southern border wall.

A national voting law is enacted requiring strict and uniform voter identification for all federal elections. The bill also includes repeal of the statute prohibiting at large House elections for any state with multiple members. Many GOP states are eager to take advantage of the repeal, believing their House delegations could be entirely Republican under the new law. With this change, all House candidates would be voted on by everyone in each of those states. There will be no single member districts. Overall, forecasters believe the GOP will net ten or more seats, based on 2024 results. In GOP states voters will elect only Republicans and in Democratic states, only Democrats.

MARCH: In a move coordinated with the national GOP, Texas Republicans in Austin introduce a bill to divide the state into four additional states, as authorized by the 1845 admission Texas to the union. Democrats denounce the move as a naked power grab, designed to keep the US Senate perpetually in GOP hands. Backers say adding the new states will make Texas "five times as great as before." Despite some Republican dissenters, the Texas legislature narrowly passes the bill, and the four new states petition Congress for admission to join the union.

APRIL: Congress passes a measure which bans abortions, for any reason, in the United States. A federal agency the "Unborn Life Protection Administration" is launched to enforce the new law. Federal marshals are hired and deployed to defiant cities where abortions are still openly performed. Dramatically, Democratic governor Gavin Newsom (CA) stands at the door of an abortion clinic in Sacramento and is arrested. The action, or stunt, echoes Alabama Governor George Wallace's 1963 performance at the University of Alabama.

MAY: The "2025 Jobs Creation and Tax Reduction Act" is passed and signed into law. The bill lowers capital gains and income tax rates by 10% across the board, retroactive to January 1.

JUNE: There are mass arrests of doctors and nurses at illegally operating abortion clinics throughout the nation. Arrests are often met with resistance, some are violent. Twelve federal marshals are shot and two are killed.

JULY: The Affordable Health Care Act (a.k.a., Obamacare) is repealed. Millions lose access to government subsidized plans. Medicaid expansion is also eliminated for the 37 states which had accepted it. Nationwide, Democrats vigorously protest and swiftly file court appeals.

AUGUST: Several new "left-wing terrorist organization" are identified by the FBI. They pledge the overthrow of "the fascist pig Republican regime". One group offers bounties, to be paid in crypto currency, for the assassination of any GOP senator or representative. Another, operating from Cuba (perhaps with Chinese or Iranian funding), advertises a $100,000,000 reward *para la cabeza de Trump*.

SEPTEMBER: The "2025 Sedition and Rebellion Act" becomes law targeting even those who express disagreement with the government. Although supposedly aimed at terrorists, the new statute could place even peaceful critics under arrest.

OCTOBER: Five states in the South pass laws which restrict access to all birth control pills and devices. Three states prohibit their use by those who are unmarried, regardless of age.

NOVEMBER: The four new Texas states elect six GOP senators and two Democrats. The Senate now becomes 60 Republicans and 48 Democrats.

DECEMBER: The US military deploys 30,000 army troops to the US/Mexico border. They will reinforce the thinly stretched Border Patrol in areas where no wall has been built.

# 2026

JANUARY: Trump declares January 6 as a "Day of National Remembrance" for the patriots, who in 2021, tried to prevent the 2020 presidential election from being stolen. He pardons all convicted for their actions and awards each a special freedom medal in a White House ceremony.

FEBRUARY: The "Civil Service Reform Act of 2026" allows the administration to replace tenured federal bureaucrats with political appointees. Thousands of employees are fired, and their jobs filled by Republican loyalists. The US Commerce Secretary pledges that the 2030 Census Questionnaire "will expose millions of illegal aliens living in the country."

MARCH: The Taft-Hartley Act of 1947 is modified creating a "national right to work law." This impacts not just private employment, but as importantly, public employees who will no longer be required to pay union dues to work for any governmental entity. Independent contractor law is revised as well. The revision allows employers to classify millions more workers as non-employees, ineligible for unemployment benefits if laid-off, or terminated.

APRIL: The US Secretary of Energy reopens Biden-era restricted areas to oil drilling, declaring that "America must shed the shackles of foreigners and become energy independent once again." The budget of the Environmental Protection Administration is reduced by 65%. All federal agencies are forbidden to use the words "climate change" in any statements.

MAY: By the end of the month, 14 states have passed laws to define marriage as that between a man and a woman. There are numerous lawsuits initiated when gay couples are denied marital rights.

JUNE: The Supreme Court affirms the national abortion ban. Several attempts are made to assassinate GOP appointed justices and one is seriously injured in a bomb blast.

JULY: A new "American Citizenship" law is passed by Congress. It denies birth-right citizenship to those children who are born of illegal immigrants. The new law is immediately challenged by those representing "undocumented residents of the United States."

AUGUST: Ukraine, shorn of US funding, agrees to Vladimir Putin's terms and formally cedes the territories annexed by Russia in 2022. It also promises not to attempt to join the European Union or NATO. Former Ukraine leader Zelensky departs and settles in Britain.

SEPTEMBER: A national concealed weapon law is passed by Congress which voids requirements for a state permit or training, for anyone lawfully owning a gun.

OCTOBER: Donald Trump's approval ratings average 43%. The race for Congress is close, with Democrats slightly in the lead.

NOVEMBER: Despite winning 52% of the House vote, Democrats gain just seven seats. New at-large elections are blamed for the poor showing. There is no net change in the Senate, but the GOP loses three governorships. Two other Democratic gubernatorial wins are overturned by state GOP legislatures. Off year voter participation continues to decline. Only 41% vote in 2026, down from 47% in 2022 and 49% in 2018.

DECEMBER: Retiring Senator Mitch McConnell is replaced as GOP Majority Leader by John Thune (SD) who promises "full steam ahead on the conservative agenda."

# 2027

JANUARY: The "Saving Social Security and Medicare Bill" is enacted. It raises the age for receiving partial Social Security benefits to 65 (was 62), full benefits to 70 (was 67) and the maximum benefits to 73 (was 70). Lifetime Medicare payouts are limited to $100,000. Only people born in 1978 and after will be affected by the changes. Republicans claim, "these minor modifications will save our healthcare system from bankruptcy."

Three incumbent Republican House members, who lost close reelection bids by under 1,000 votes are seated by the GOP majority. Each maintains that "Democrat fraud" caused their defeats.

FEBRUARY: The economy continues to improve. Despite a $1.9 billion deficit, inflation retreats to 3.5%. The Federal Reserve lowers the prime rate to 3.75%. The Dow-Jones Industrial Average, after tumbling by more than 30% in 2022-23, is now steadily rising.

MARCH: Congress passes the "1st Amendment Security Act." The bill purports to ensure "the freedom of true information throughout the United States." The law prohibits the internet from banning the accounts of any "public figure, past, present or future" who could be registered on their sites. Further, it penalizes "speaking slanderously against the leadership of the nation" with fines of up to $10,000 per offense. Civil libertarians decry this law, saying it could turn the country into a tyranny.

APRIL: China imposes a naval blockade on Taiwan, effectively preventing that island from exporting or importing products by sea.

MAY: The "Liberty Home Schoolers' Bill" awards $2500 per year in federal tax credits for each student in kindergarten through grade 12, educated at home by a parent or legal guardian. GOP congressional supporters say it will save local taxpayers millions each year by reducing burdensome and unnecessary enrollments in public schools. Opponents counter that the law undermines the American educational system. It will only produce, they say, hundreds of thousands of poorly taught semi-literates unprepared for any higher education.

JUNE: The US Supreme Court combining several cases, upholds the right of states to forbid same sex marriages.

JULY: Leading Democratic candidates for the 2028 nomination are Senators Tammy Duckworth (IL), Alex Padilla (CA), Raphael Warnock (GA), former Vice-President Kamala Harris (CA), plus former US Transportation Secretary Pete Buttigieg (IN). US Representative Alexandria Ocasio-Cortez of NY (now of legal age to be president), also declares her candidacy, but hints she might run as a Democratic Socialist if denied the nomination.

AUGUST: Donald Trump Jr. announces his candidacy for the 2028 presidential election. Other GOPer's enter, including Vice-President Elise Stefanik, Senator Ted Cruz (TX), Governor Ron DeSantis (FL) and Senator Marco Rubio (FL).

SEPTEMBER: The "Promotion of Free Speech and Religious Liberty Act" is passed. Modeled after the Trump Executive Order of 2017, it ends the prohibition on churches from endorsing or contributing funds to political candidates or causes. Leaders of Protestant Fundamentalist denominations rejoice.

OCTOBER: The "2027 Jobs Creation and Tax Act" lowers income and capital gain tax rates by another 10%. The Estate Tax (a.k.a. Death Tax) is completely repealed as are sunset provisions for past tax reduction laws.

NOVEMBER: Referendums are held in five blue states to succeed from the United States. In three the measure passes: California, Oregon, and Washington. Successionist leaders talk of uniting them to bring forth "The Western Social Democratic Commonwealth of North America."

DECEMBER: Republicans in eastern parts of those seceded states organize to oppose succession. They appeal to Congress, asking it to admit their breakaway sections as the new states of East California, East Oregon, and East Washington.

# US CONSTITUTION

The United States ratified the Constitution in 1789. It replaced the Articles of Confederation. As originally adopted, the Constitution had just ten amendments, called the Bill of Rights. Since then, 17 more were added and one was repealed (Prohibition). The Supreme Court is the final arbiter. It can decide, usually after a long appeals process, whether a decision by a lower court should stand or not, based on its "constitutionality." The Supreme Court hears very few appeals and overturns even fewer.

Some rulings have been momentous, fundamentally changing American society: Roe v. Wade (1973) and Brown v. Topeka Kansas Board of Education (1954). Supreme Court members are partisan political appointees, now more than ever before. Their future rulings are likely to reshape America as much as those did in the last century.

Listed below are the 27 amendments with commentary on how and what might change under an upcoming Republican administration.

## 1ST AMENDMENT (1789)

"Congress shall make no law respecting an establishment of religion or prohibiting the free exercise thereof; or abridging the freedom of speech, or of the press; or the right of people peaceably to assemble, and to petition the Government for a redress of grievances."

Commentary: At issue now are political spending limits and liable laws. Potentially some of the events of January 6, 2021, might be interpreted as a "redress of grievances."

## 2ND AMENDMENT (1789)

"A well-regulated Militia, being necessary to the security of a free state, the right of the people to keep and bear arms, shall not be infringed."

Commentary: At the forefront in 2023 are conceal and carry gun laws. Also, if any gun permit is needed to buy a weapon and if back-ground checks can be enforced. What might be most at issue in the future is which types of weapons are allowable for personal ownership.

## 3RD AMENDMENT (1789)

"No soldier shall, in time of peace be quartered in any house without the consent of the owner, nor in time of war, but in a manner to be prescribed by law."

Commentary: No court review is expected.

## 4TH AMENDMENT (1789)

"The right of the people to be secure in their persons, houses, papers, and effects, against unreasonable search and seizures, shall not be violated, and no warrants shall issue, but upon probable cause, supported by oath or affirmations, and particularly describing the place to be searched, and the person or things to be seized."

Commentary: No court review is expected, despite the FBI's Mar-A-Lago raid on Donald Trump's golf club and residence.

## 5TH AMENDMENT (1789)

"No person shall be held to answer for a capital, or otherwise infamous crime, unless on a presentment or indictment of a Grand Jury, except in cases arising in the land or naval forces, or in the Militia, when in actual service in time of War or public danger; nor shall any person be subject for the same offense to be twice put in jeopardy of life or limb; nor shall be compelled in any criminal case to be a witness against himself, nor be deprived of life, liberty, or property, without the due process of law; nor shall private property be taken for public use, without just compensation."

Commentary: The search and seizure section may be re-examined concerning law enforcement agencies' taking property from suspected felons without payment. That may violate the due process of law.

## 6TH AMENDMENT (1789)

"In all criminal prosecutions, the accused shall enjoy the right to a speedy and public trial, by an impartial jury of the state and district wherein the crime shall been committed, which district shall have been previously ascertained by law, and to be informed of the nature and cause of the accusation; to be confronted with witnesses against him; to have compulsory process for obtaining witnesses in his favor, and to the assistance of counsel for his defense."

Commentary: No review is expected, although speedy trials rarely happen nowadays and could be a basis for lawsuits.

## 7TH AMENDMENT (1789)

"In suits of common law, where the value in controversy shall exceed twenty dollars, the right to trial by jury shall be preserved, and no fact tried by a jury, shall be otherwise re-examined in any court of the United States than according to the rules of common law."

Commentary: No review is expected.

## 8TH AMENDMENT (1789)

"Excessive bail shall not be required, nor excessive fines imposed, nor cruel and unusual punishments inflicted."

Commentary: In 1972 the Supreme Court suspended the death penalty saying it violated the 8th Amendment. Since then, most states revised their laws to address the reasons for the court's ruling, but very few executions have taken place. Meanwhile left-leaning jurisdictions have reduced or sometimes eliminated cash bail. Expect challenges from those seeking to get tougher on criminals and suspects.

## 9TH AMENDMENT (1789)

"The enumeration in the Constitution, of certain rights, shall not be construed to deny or disparage others retained by the people."

Commentary: No court review is expected.

## 10TH AMENDMENT (1789)

"The powers not delegated to the United States by the Constitution, nor prohibited by it to the states, are reserved to states respectively, or to the people."

Commentary: No court review is expected. The 10th Amendment reiterates the 9th but adds the states as well as the people.

## 11TH AMENDMENT (1794)

"The judicial power of the United States shall not be construed to extend to any suit in law or equity, commenced or prosecuted against one of the United States by citizens of another state, or by citizens or subjects of any foreign state."

Commentary: No review is expected, but this Amendment has generated multiple cases in multiple centuries decided by the Supreme Court.

## 12TH AMENDMENT (1804)

"The electors shall meet in their respective states and vote by ballot for President and Vice-President, one of whom, at least, shall not be an inhabitant of the same state with themselves; they shall name in their ballots the person voted for as President and in distinct ballots the person voted for as Vice-President, and they shall make distinct lists of all persons voted for as President, and the number of votes for each, which lists they shall sign and certify, and transmit sealed to the seat of Government of the United States, directed to the President of the Senate.

"The President of the Senate shall, in the presence of the Senate and House of Representatives, open all the certificates and the votes shall then be counted.

"The person having the greatest number of votes for President, shall be the President, if such numbers be a majority of the whole number of electors appointed; and if no person have such a majority, then from the persons having the highest number not exceeding three on the list of those voted for as President, the House of Representatives shall choose immediately, by ballot, the President.

"But in choosing the President, the votes shall be taken by states, the representation from each state having one vote; a quorum for this purpose shall consist of a member or members from two-thirds of the states, and majority of all states shall be necessary to a choice.

"And if the House of Representatives shall not choose a President whenever the right shall devolve on them, before the fourth day of March next following, then the Vice-President shall act as in the case of the death or other constitutional disability of the President.

"The person having the greatest number of votes as Vice-President, shall be Vice-President, if such number be a majority of the whole number of electors appointed, and if no person has a majority, then two from the highest numbers on the list, the Senate shall choose the Vice-President; a quorum for the purpose shall consist of two-thirds of the whole number of Senators, and a majority of the whole number shall be necessary to a choice. But no person constitutionally ineligible to the office of President shall be eligible to that of Vice-President of the United States."

Commentary: Modified by the 20th Amendment and no review is expected.

# 13TH AMENDMENT (1865)

"Neither slavery nor involuntary servitude, except as a punishment for crime whereof the party shall have been duly convicted, shall exist within the United States, or any place subject to their jurisdiction. Congress shall have the power to enforce this article by appropriate legislation."

Commentary: No review is expected.

# 14TH AMENDMENT (1868)

"All persons born or naturalized in the United States, and subject to the jurisdiction thereof, are citizens of the United States and of the state wherein they reside. No state shall make or enforce any law which shall abridge the privileges or immunities of citizens of the United States; nor shall deprive any person of life, liberty, or property, without due process of law; nor deny to any person within its jurisdiction the equal protection of the law.

"Representatives shall be apportioned among the several states according to their respective numbers, counting the whole numbers, excluding Indians not taxed. But when the right to vote at any election for the choice of electors for President and Vice-President of the United States, Representatives in Congress, the Executive and Judicial officers of a State, or members of the Legislature thereof, is denied to any male inhabitants of such states, being twenty-one years of age, and citizens of the United States, in any way abridged, except for participation in rebellion, or other crime, the basis of representation therein shall be reduced in the proportion which the number of such male citizens shall bear to the whole number of male citizens twenty-one years of age in such state.

"No person shall be a Senator or Representative in Congress, or elector of President or Vice-President, or hold any office, civil or military, under the United States, or any state, who, having previously taken an oath, as a member of Congress, or an officer of the United States, or as a member of any State legislature executive or judicial officer of any State, to support the Constitution of the United States, shall have engaged in insurrection or rebellion against the same, or given aid or comfort to the enemies thereof. But Congress, by a vote of two-thirds of each House, may remove such disability.

"The validity of the public debt of the United States, authorized by law, including debts incurred for payment of pensions and bounties for services in suppressing insurrection or rebellion, shall not be questioned. But neither the United States nor any state shall assume or pay any debt or obligation incurred in aid of insurrection or rebellion against the United States, or any claim for the loss or emancipation of any slave; but all such debts, obligations and claims shall be held illegal and void.

Congress shall have the power to enforce, by appropriate legislation, the provisions of this article."

Commentary: Some have speculated that Donald Trump could be excluded from the winning the presidency in 2024 having engaged in an act in rebellion on January 6, 2021. That is a very high wall to scale and unlikely that the Supreme Court would act before the 2024 election.

## 15TH AMENDMENT (1870)

"The right of citizens of the United States to vote shall not be denied or abridged by the United States or by any state on account of race, color, or previous condition of servitude.

"The Congress shall have the power to enforce this article by appropriate legislation."

Commentary: No review is expected. From the end of Reconstruction, beginning in 1877 until 1965, the voting rights of Black citizens in the Old Confederacy were eroded or disappeared entirely.

## 16TH AMENDMENT (1913)

"The Congress shall have the power to lay and collect taxes on incomes, from whatever source derived, without apportionment among the several States, without regard to census or enumeration."

Commentary: No review is expected. The 16th Amendment is the cornerstone of modern-day federal funding. Before then the government relied on a hodgepodge of revenues. Would Supreme Court Justices expect their salaries to be paid by the tariff?

# 17TH AMENDMENT (1913)

"The Senate of the United States shall be composed of two Senators from each state, elected by the people thereof, for six years; and each Senator shall have one vote. The electors of each State shall have the qualifications requisite for electors of the most numerous branches of the state legislatures.

"When vacancies happen in the representation of any state in the Senate, the executive authority of such state shall issue writs of election to fill such vacancies. Provided that the legislature of any state may empower thereof to make temporary appointments until the people fill the vacancies by election as the legislature may direct.

"This amendment shall not be construed as to affect the election or term of any Senator chosen before it becomes valid as part of the Constitution."

Commentary: No review is expected. Repeal of the 17th amendment was a minor conservative cause some years ago. It could be again if a new Constitutional Convention were called.

# 18TH AMENDMENT (1919)

"After one year from the ratification of this article the manufacture, sale, or transportation of intoxicating liquors within, the importation thereof into, or the exportation thereof from the United States and all territory subject to the jurisdiction thereof for beverage purposes is hereby prohibited.

"The Congress and several states shall have concurrent power to enforce this article by appropriate legislation.

"This article shall be inoperative unless it shall have been ratified as an amendment to the Constitution by the legislatures of several states, as provided in the Constitution, within seven years from the date of the submission hereof to the states by Congress."

Commentary: The 18th Amendment was repealed by the 21st Amendment.

# 19TH AMENDMENT (1920)

"The right of citizens of the United States to vote shall not be denied or abridged by the United States or any state on account of sex.

"Congress shall have power to enforce this article by appropriate legislation."

Commentary: No review is expected.

# 20TH AMENDMENT (1933)

"The terms of the President and the Vice-President shall end at noon on the 20th day of January, and the terms of Senators and Representatives at noon on the 3rd day of January, of the years in which such terms would have ended if this article had not been ratified; and the terms of their successors shall then begin.

"The Congress shall assemble at least once every year, and such meetings shall begin at noon on the 3rd day of January, unless they shall by law appoint a different day.

"If, at the time fixed for the beginning of the term of President, the President elect shall have died, the Vice-President elect shall become President. If a President shall not have been chosen before the time fixed for the beginning of the term, or if the President elect shall have failed to qualify, then the Vice-President elect shall act as President until a President shall have qualified. The Congress may by law provide for the case wherein neither a President nor a Vice-President elect shall have qualified, declaring who shall then act as President, or the manner in which one who is to act shall be elected, and such person shall act accordingly until a President or Vice – President shall have qualified.

"The Congress may by law provide for the case of the death of any persons from whom the House of Representatives may choose a President whenever the right of choice shall have devolved upon them, and the case of the death of any of the persons from whom the Senate may choose a Vice-President whenever the right of choice shall have been devolved upon them.

"Sections one and two shall take effect on the 15th day of October following the ratification of this article.

"This article shall be inoperative unless it shall have been ratified as an amendment to the Constitution by the legislatures of three-fourths of the several states within seven years from the date of its submission."

Commentary: No review is expected.

# 21ST AMENDMENT (1933)

"The 18th article of amendment to the Constitution of the United States is hereby repealed.

"This article shall be inoperative unless it shall have been ratified as an amendment to the Constitution by conventions of the several states, as provided in the Constitution, within seven years from the date of submission hereof to the states by Congress."

Commentary: No review is expected.

# 22ND AMENDMENT (1951)

"No person shall be elected to the office of the President more than twice, and no person who has held the office of President, or acted as President, for more than two years of a term which some other person was elected President shall be elected to the office of the President more than once. But this article shall not apply to any person holding the office President when this article was proposed by the Congress and shall prevent any person who may be holding the office of President, or acting as President, during the term within which this article becomes operative from holding the office of President or acting as President during the remainder of such term.

"This article shall be inoperative unless it shall be ratified as an amendment to the Constitution by the legislatures of three-fourths of the several states within seven years from the date of its submission to the States by Congress."

Commentary: No review is expected.

## 23RD AMENDMENT (1961)

"The District of Columbia constituting the seat of Government of the United States shall appoint in such manner as the Congress may direct.

"A number of electors of President and Vice-President to equal the whole number of Senators and Representatives in Congress to which the district would be entitled if it were a state, but in no event more than the least populous state. They shall be in addition to those appointed by the States, but they shall be considered, for purposes of the election of President and Vice-President, to be electors appointed by the state; and shall meet in the district and perform such duties as provided by the 12th article of amendment.

"The Congress shall have power to enforce this by appropriate legislation."

Commentary: No review is expected.

## 24TH AMENDMENT (1964)

"The right of citizens of the United States to vote in any primary or other election for President or Vice-President, or for Senator or Representative in Congress, shall not be denied or abridged by the United States or any state by reason of failure to pay poll or other tax.

"The Congress shall power to enforce this article by appropriate legislation."

Commentary: No review is expected. There is a possible loophole, dividing voting by federal versus state elections. But no state may attempt that and present the Supreme Court with an appeal to decide.

## 25TH AMENDMENT (1967)

"In case of the removal of the President from office or his death or resignation, the Vice – President shall become President.

"Whenever there is a vacancy in the office of Vice-President, the President shall nominate a Vice-President who shall take office upon the confirmation by a majority vote of both Houses of Congress.

"Whenever the President transmits to the President pro tempore of the Senate and the Speaker of the House of Representatives his written declaration that he is unable to discharge the powers and duties of his office, and until he transmits to them a written declaration to the contrary, such powers and duties shall be discharged by the Vice-President as Acting President.

"Whenever the Vice-President and a majority of either the principal officers of the executive departments or of such other body as Congress may by law provide, transmit to the President pro tempore of the Senate and Speaker of the House of Representatives their written declaration that the President is unable to discharge the powers and duties of his office, the Vice-President immediately shall assume the powers and duties of the of the office as Acting President.

"Thereafter, when the President transmits the President pro tempore of the Senate the Speaker of the House of Representatives his written declaration that no inability exists, he shall resume the powers and duties of his office unless the Vice-President and a majority of either the principal officers of the executive department or other such body as Congress may by law provide, transmit within four days to the President pro tempore of the Senate and the Speaker of the House of Representatives their written declaration that the President is unable to discharge the powers and duties of his office. Thereupon Congress shall decide the issue, assembling within forty-eight hours for that purpose if not in session. If the Congress, within twenty-one days after the receipt of the latter written declaration, or, if Congress is not in session, within twenty-one days after Congress is required to assemble, determines by two-thirds of the vote of both Houses that President is unable to discharge the powers and duties of his office, the Vice-President shall continue to discharge the same as Acting President; otherwise, the President shall resume the powers and duties of his office."

Commentary: No review is expected. There was speculation – mostly out of left field in both senses – during Trump's 1st term, that the amendment could be used to place Vice-President Pence in the Oval Office.

## 26TH AMENDMENT (1971)

"The right of citizens of the United States who are eighteen years of age, or older, to vote shall not be denied or abridged by the United States or by any state on account of age.

"The Congress shall have the power to enforce this article by appropriate legislation."

Commentary: No review is expected.

## 27TH AMENDMENT (1992)

"No law, varying the compensation for the services of the Senators and Representatives, shall take effect, until an election shall have intervened."

Commentary: No review is expected.

# KEY SUPREME COURT DECISIONS

Listed below are key cases which the Supreme Court decided in the past 70 years. What are the chances that they will be modified or overturned?

- MAPP v. OHIO (1961): Search and Seizure. Are illegal police searches and seizures (without obtaining prior court approvals) allowable as evidence? The opinion stated that all evidence obtained in violation of the 4th Amendment is not admissible in state courts. Since then, many other cases have appeared before the high Court, often involving police searches in traffic stops.

    Expected change: Probable expansion of the right of the police to conduct searches. But that may not extend to the admissibility of evidence obtained without a warrant.

- BAKER v. CARR (1962): Equally populated voting districts are mandated for local elections. This was one of the most transformational cases that the Earl Warren led Court decided. An earlier high Court said (Colegrove v. Green, 1946) that the political nature of apportionment precluded judicial intervention. In 1964 the Court further ruled in Wesberry v. Sanders (US House of Representatives districting) and Reynolds v. Sims (state legislative districting). These rulings required both the US House and state legislative bodies to create districts of equal populations. This was called the principle of "one man one vote". Subsequent rulings also required fair representation of minority voters, first Black and later Hispanic.

    Expected change: The high Court may allow more flexibility in what defines an equally populated district. The current rule of thumb says that within 5% of absolute equality is acceptable. More significantly, it may determine that non-citizens need not be counted.

- MILLER v. CALIFORNIA (1973): Obscenity. What constitutes pornography or obscenity? The Court changed the definition from content "utterly without socially redeeming value" to that which lacks "serious literary, artistic, political, or scientific value." The ruling eventually led to many states striking down the criminalization of obscenity and allowing the free flow of magazines, films, and other forms of adult entertainment.

  Expected change: States and localities could be given more latitude in banning of so called obscene printed materials, movies, and internet sites.

- GRISWOLD v. CONNECTICUT (1965): Birth Control and the "right to privacy". This decision foreshadowed Roe v. Wade. A Connecticut law passed in 1879 forbade "the use of any drug, medical device or other instrument in furthering contraception." The head of Connecticut Planned Parenthood was the defendant. At issue was the right to marital privacy against state restrictions against couples' being counseled on the use of contraceptives.

  Expected change: States might once again be allowed to ban the sale of contraceptives.

- BRADY v. MARYLAND (1963): Suppression of evidence by the state (i.e., its prosecutors) at a defendant's capital crime trial. The Supreme Court held that the suppression denied defendant the due process clause of the 14th Amendment and remanded the case.

  Expected change: The case might be revisited and overturned, at least in part. Most conservative Justices then on the high Court voted against the decision.

- MIRANDA v. ARIZONA (1966): Defendants must be told their rights during a police interrogation. "You have the right to remain silent and refuse to answer questions." Anyone watching a TV show or movie in the last 50 years is familiar with that line. But before the Miranda court decision, those arrested usually did not hear it. In a narrow five to four ruling, the high Court held Miranda had been denied his rights granted by the 5th Amendment.

  Expected change: A conservative high Court is likely to hold that there is no constitutional requirement to specifically inform those arrested of their rights.

- FURMAN v. GEORGIA (1972): Death penalty law was overturned by the Supreme Court as violating the 8th and 14th Amendments. In response, states began revising their laws in response to the ruling. In 1977 executions resumed, beginning with self-confessed killer Gary Gilmore. Although there is a federal statute for the death penalty, it seldom has been exercised. Donald Trump resumed those executions after a hiatus under Barack Obama. Almost all death sentences are imposed by the states, however. But capital punishment is now outlawed in most of them. Still the death penalty is popular with the public, by a roughly two to one margin.

  Expected change: States with capital punishment will execute more prisoners on death row and perhaps add new capital offenses. The high Court will probably continue to refuse to overturn most death sentence appeals.

- ROE v. WADE (1973): The 2020 Dobbs decision overturned Roe v. Wade.

  Expected change: More states will enact more restrictions, including outright abortion prohibitions. The Supreme Court will likely uphold all of them.

- US v. NIXON (1974): Executive privilege. This determined the right of a sitting US president to withhold information from other government branches to preserve confidential communications. The case related to the "Watergate Tapes," which Richard Nixon made and were the subject of a Congressional subpoena. The Supreme Court ruled there was a limited immunity in areas of diplomatic or military affairs. However, it said that this did not apply to Nixon's case. Shortly afterwards, Nixon became the first US president to resign.

    Expected change: The high Court may decide that executive privilege extends to any information which a president chooses to withhold, perhaps even after the end of his or her presidency.

- LAWRENCE v. TEXAS (2003): Same sex relations. The Supreme Court overturned a Texas conviction by a vote of six to three. It said the Texas statute violated the due process clause of the 14th Amendment. Of the three dissenting Justices (all Republican appointees), only Clarence Thomas remains on the high Court.

    Expected change: Conservative states may pass new laws again criminalizing gay sex. The Supreme Court may uphold them.

- OBERGEFELL v. HODGES (2015): Same sex marriage. The Supreme Court narrowly overturned all state laws forbidding same sex couples to marry.

    Expected change: Conservative states will likely pass statutes defining marriage as that between a man and woman, not between same sex couples. The high Court will likely allow those to stand.

- DISTRICT OF COLUMBIA v. HELLER (2010): Guns rights. The Supreme Court upheld gun ownership within homes, even if a gun was unlicensed. In 2012 it further ruled in McDonald v. Chicago, that the 2nd Amendment protected individuals against governmental infringement of the right to possess a handgun for self-defense.

In 2022 the Court struck down a New York state law that required strict licensing for individuals to carry guns outside their homes.

Expected change: Exactly what limitations the Supreme Court might accept, if any, will be found in upcoming cases as other state and local statutes are challenged. Might it decide that the carrying of any weapons, concealed or not, even without a permit is lawful? Will we see heavily armed men with AR-15 assault rifles roaming freely throughout the streets, stores, restaurants, and schools of America? Maybe we will.

- CITIZENS UNITED v. FEDERAL ELECTIONS COMMISSION (2010): Campaign contributions by corporations. The Supreme Court that ruled corporations have the same 1st Amendment rights as individuals and therefore cannot be limited in their political spending. Many other rulings before and after 2010 involved Federal Election Commission (FEC) spending rules.

Expected change: There likely will be further litigation to enable more money to be spent outside the current limitations. The Supreme Court would probably rule favorably. Or the Gordian knot of endless lawsuits may be cut, and the FEC abolished by Congress with the approval of a GOP president.

- SHELBY COUNTY, TENNESEE v. HOLDER (2011): States with a low 1964 election turnout rate were required to have their voting laws "pre-cleared" (i.e., approved) by the federal government, as stated in Section IV of the 1965 Voting Rights Act. Conservatives in states effected, mostly in the old Confederacy, complained. The Supreme Court, under Chief Justice John Roberts, ruled five to four that Section IV was unconstitutional. Each of the Court's Democratic appointees dissented. Since then, many of those states have altered their voting laws. Democrats in turn complained, saying the new laws reduced voting participation by minorities, especially Blacks.

Expected change: Conservative states will continue to enact alleged "voting barriers" to which Democrats will object. However, the high Court is unlikely to object to their lawfulness. A GOP initiated federal voting law may well come before the Supreme Court in 2025 or after.